AUG 2 9 2001

WITHDRAWN

DATE		
LLOYD TABER-MARINA DEL REY LIBRARY		
COUNTY OF LOS ANGELES PUBLIC LIBRARY		
4533 Admiralty Way		
Marina del Rey, CA 90292		
(310) 821-3415		

334

BAKER & TAYLOR

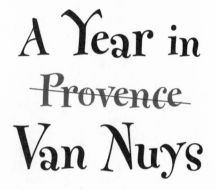

A Year in ~~Provence~~ Van Nuys

A Year in ~~Provence~~ Van Nuys

Sandra Tsing Loh

Crown Publishers / New York

●

For the ever-glamorous and not always fictional Tatjana Peng Loh

●

Photograph of Bert Lahr courtesy of Photofest.

Published by Crown Publishers, New York, New York.
Member of the Crown Publishing Group.

Random House, Inc. New York, Toronto, London, Sydney, Auckland
www.randomhouse.com

Crown is a trademark and the Crown colophon is a registered trademark
of Random House, Inc.

Printed in the United States of America

Design by Barbara Sturman

Library of Congress Cataloging-in-Publication Data
Loh, Sandra Tsing.
A year in Van Nuys / by Sandra Tsing Loh.
1. Van Nuys (Los Angeles, Calif.)—Social life and customs—Humor.
2. Los Angeles (Calif.)—Social life and customs—Humor.
3. Loh, Sandra Tsing.   4. Loh, Sandra Tsing—Homes and haunts—
California—Los Angeles.   5. Van Nuys (Los Angeles, Calif.)—
Biography.   6. Los Angeles (Calif.)—Biography.   I. Title.
F869.L86 V44   2001
979.4′94—dc21   00-050886
ISBN 0-609-60812-6

10 9 8 7 6 5 4 3 2
First Edition

Midway along the journey of our life
	I woke to find myself in some dark woods,
	for I had wandered off from the straight path.

How hard it is to tell what it was like,
	this wood of wilderness, savage and stubborn
	(the thought of it brings back all my old fears),

a bitter place! Death could scarce be bitterer.
	But if I would show the good that came of it
	I must talk about things other than the good.

Inferno, by Dante Alighieri ✳

✳Age thirty-five

"Van Nuys was just this furnace that could destroy any creative thought that managed to creep into your mind."

●

Robert Redford, actor, Van Nuys High graduate

●

The Winter
of Our
Discontent

January 1

11:47 a.m.

Temperature: 83 degrees

Van Nuys, California
My Bedroom

●

After Having Just Finished

Peter Mayle's *A Year in Provence*

and a Tupperwareful

of Zone-Approved Nonfat Turkey

●

The View from
My Window

Recently I've started coming out of denial over the fact that I do not live in Provence. Not only do I not live in Provence, I do not even live in a nice part of Los Angeles.

It's true that when we first moved to Van Nuys—this ethnically mixed, upper-lower-middle-class suburb in the sun-swept grid of the San Fernando Valley—it didn't seem such a hellish place to live. My hand-painted Italian ceramic coffee cup rattled in its saucer but once a month due to wheeling police helicopters. The night sky—smoggy, starless, nougat-hued, flamed by a million Burger King signs—was so bright in summer you could actually read by it. With ever more *carnicerías, taquerías,* and *pupuserías* opening daily, with no effort one could become both bilingual and an expert on pork products, and I celebrated that knowledge.

I will admit that—in contrast to Provence—the sudden shriek of a rooster in the dead of the afternoon tended not to be a welcome sound. Particularly when one was sitting at one's (Ikea, but by no means the cheapest thing at Ikea) desk in one's neatly appointed home office in the middle of what one had thought was an upwardly mobile L.A. neighborhood. The lawns somewhat balding, yes, the houses perhaps a bit *too* gaily painted, every third or fourth bungalow the color of eye-piercing sorbet—lime green, raspberry cream, banana yellow. . . .

I'm not trying to be elitist here. I'm not trying to be classist. All I'm saying is that at the time we bought this, our tiny, "swamp-cooled" ranch-style house, which was in 1991, near the top of the Southern California real-estate market (and I'm not even mentioning our ticking-clock/uranium fission/Jerry Bruckheimer–type loan, with balloon payments swelling suddenly into a boil and bursting mushroom cloud–like in the year 2014) . . . Anyway, all I'm saying is that at the time of the procurement of the title deed of this particular lot, within a two-hundred-foot radius of the property lines, to my knowledge, there were no chickens.

Of course, then came the tsunami of Bad Media Tidings *about* our bravely tattered little neighborhood. The bombshell that Van Nuys is regularly ranked one of the ten worst neighborhoods to live in in Los Angeles (courtesy of *Los Angeles* magazine), L.A. itself considered one of the ten worst cities to live in in the nation (courtesy of *Fortune*). The caravan of production semis rolling onto our street to film an episode of the glamorous new Aaron Spelling show *Models, Inc.* . . . my smugness turning to horror at the news that our block's most resplendent Victorian three-story had been cast as the tumbledown shack of the "grungy" model's crazy musician boyfriend who wanted to kill her.

You'd think maybe we could get some counterculture *avant-garde art* points for living in such a dangerous—and yet vibrantly creative—neighborhood, a kind of . . . Hell's Kitchen of the West Coast. Because, after all, Ben and I are artists (he's a musician, I'm a writer) (or at least I used to be a writer) (I used to be a writer when I was actually still writing my novel) (even now, the thought of it brings a wave of heaviness—must suppress). . . . Anyway, Ben and I are artists, so why shouldn't we live in a vibrant, dangerous neighborhood, with graffiti, gunshots, roving gangs who swagger and flash hand signals and groove on down to the beat of a . . . a feisty street kid drumming on a . . . an overturned white bucket. . . . (You know the one I mean? The kid in that commercial? And *Bring in Da Noise, Bring in Da Funk*? Who plays the bucket?)

But no, even our San Fernando Valley *gangs* don't match up, in Los Angeles. Echo Park: That's, apparently, where the really trend-setting—the really *seminal*—gangs are. "You have to understand that Echo Park gangs have a whole unique semiotics," this nasal-voiced blonde told me recently at a party. She was one of those Echo Park USC film-school types who's donned a saggy old Allison Anders dress and suddenly considers herself an expert on gang life. She felt our Van Nuys gangs were somehow too sleepy, too indolent, there is too much convenient parking. "Excuse me, Meredith," I snapped, "but you are *not* an Echo Park *loca* and never will be! You're from Portland." She turned white. See how ugly? Can't we all just get along?

At any rate, as I ponder all these things on a sweltering New Year's Day at this, my semi-advanced/waist-deep-in-my-thirties/been-through-the-rat-race/regrets-I've-had-a-few/etc., stage in life, I admit that this is extremely confusing to me, the disconnect between it, my home, and me, the person. I mean, I'm the sort of person who should by now, in this second act of a well if quietly lived life, be growing my own basil and remodeling a falling-down (but exquisite, charming) rustic farmhouse, if not in Provence, at the very least in ~~Santa Fe~~ (no—too cliché, too tacky New Age, too touristy)

~~Seattle~~ (forget it—Microsoft billionaires inflating property values right through the roof, ex—college roommate Carl lives there with wife Sumiko and devilspawn Kimmy and Timmy, their smug e-mails/garish website photos of self-designed four-thousand-square-foot home annoy)—

No, wait. I have it. I am the sort of person who should be living in a small, charming—*hitherto undiscovered*—town in Northern California by the name of . . . let's say . . . ~~Santa Marina?~~

~~Wood's Hole?~~

Oglala Springs.

Yes. Yes. Oglala Springs.

This "Oglala Springs"—my dream town, my virtual town, my *true inner hometown,* if you will, *the town in which I should be living,* is a . . . a . . .

Wonderful, close-knit, environmentally conscious community of less than ten thousand. (Although for its small size, it has a surprisingly modern and convenient airport.) (Because Howard

Hughes used to summer here in the fifties.) (But then he quickly left—only this gorgeous, perfect little airport remains.)

Oglala Springs received its picturesque start, in the 1800s, as a gold-mining town. And yet, unlike so many others, Oglala Springs has been able to smoothly transition into politically progressive modern cityhood due to the discovery of ~~valuable copper oil tungsten brass~~ (can you even mine brass? what *is* brass?) an herb. Which has been prized for many years by the Ricola Corporation, of Switzerland. You see? That's how the money comes in. They import it from us. The Swiss do. But not in a violating way. The Ricola people do it subtly, carefully, and in a way that actually *improves* the environment—amazingly, more trees are left behind than one even started with. Something about Freon.

Speaking of things that grow, Oglala Springs is also known for making *small but wonderful* wines—a buttery Gewürzt, Parker 97 Bordeaux, plum-hued, velvet-toned, berry-rich Merlots. (Yes. This feels right. Wineries! *Small but wonderful* wineries . . .)

Also *small but wonderful* is our downtown—if you can call it that! (Punctuate with hearty laugh as one smears more savory homemade Brie onto baguette round, hands to awed—and extremely grateful—guest.) You almost hesitate to call it a "downtown," as it's a thing completely without traffic! Because *no one drives* in Oglala Springs. All our residents—the novelists, the folksingers, the artisans, the jam-makers (hemp-growers? *too* Northern California funky?)—walk or skate or bike. From our rustic lakefront homes just two minutes away (A-frames, redwood decking, skylights, hot tubs, fifteen hundred square feet for eighty thousand dollars, 10 percent down is no problem, no TRW credit check needed).

Here in Oglala Springs (also we have a fabulous cultural/human-rights record, the Native Americans make these amazing dolphin/teak/turquoise sculptures that sell for zillions so they can repopulate the—er, the denuded woodlands)

(Also our Native Americans have their own PBS station that wins all these fabulous Cable/ACE Awards, something something something Bill Moyers) . . .

Anyway, the point is, life is *slower* in Oglala Springs.

Why? Because of us. The people.

Who are we?

We are the sort of people who wouldn't think of beginning our day without stopping in for conversation, a morning poem, French Roast coffee and fresh-baked croissants at the Good Day Bakery (a historic Craftsman ~~bungalow lovingly~~ preserved)—

Lunch is typically at Joan and David's Tom and Elizabeth's, a sunny outdoor café that . . .

We always enjoy a three-hour-long afternoon siesta. . . .

"Four P.M. is Tarte Tatin Hour!"

Suddenly I'm starting to feel a little worried about our town. Something is off. Is it perhaps *too* sleepy (what with the cranberry muffins and the tiny jams and the indolence)?

Hey! Wait a minute! You know what we ~~need? A festival. Yes.~~ An annual arts festival. The Oglala Springs Shakespeare Festival (too cliché? too Ashland?) . . . the Oglala Springs Brecht Festival. No. Mark Morris Dances Oglala Springs. Something some-thing something PINA BAUSCH—

No—here's a better idea. Since we *are* in California, Oglala Springs, while small, is so sophisticated (we've got all the ameni-ties, none of the pretension, and, as mentioned, a great airport). . . . That's right, we're so rustic *but sophisticated* that even a . . . a Hollywood Celebrity could live here . . . and feel at home . . .

Uh-oh. Take care. Take care. This is a slippery slope. This is where worlds collide. You get the wrong Hollywoodite in here, and suddenly in barrels *InStyle* magazine and *Entertainment Tonight*, and it's all Demi Moore in a Land Rover! USC frat guys Jet-Skiing! MTV's Spring Break at Fort Lauderdale! The Barking Coyote Saloon!

No. No. Nothing like that. *Our* celebrity has to be the sort of introspective person who would be drawn not just to our moun-tains but to our extraordinary mountain-nestled film library. The ~~Stanley Donen D. W. Griffith~~ (must work on this, truly have absolutely no idea what I'm talking about) Film Library. That person would be ~~Robert Redford Francis Ford Coppola~~ (no, they already have Sundance and the Napa Valley, it has to be someone more obscure than that and a little less-moneyed, if equally nature-loving, pro-environmental, winery-implying) ~~Peter Coyote Ally Sheedy Ed Begley, Jr.~~ Brenda Vaccaro (BRENDA VACCARO? What kind of town would that be? "Authentic Brenda Vaccaro Blue Chile Salsa." "The Brenda Vaccaro Osprey Preserve." No).

Or perhaps an older man. Paul Newman all-natural salad dressings. Clint Eastwood: mayor of Carmel. (Jerry Brown is mayor of Oakland, but Brown seems a little shrill and Oakland a little grim.) Okay, how about Oscar-winning (but what megahits has he had *recently*—and hence how perfect for our wonderful and resolutely *small* town) Milos Forman? Doesn't that sound perfect? Don't you see him settling in Northern California and making wines? Salad dressing? Perhaps some wonderful aloe-and-lemongrass soaps?

I'm getting confused.

I think I need to make up a chart. I need to clarify the rules and boundaries, to make sure no toxic Elements get into my Biodome 2000 of . . . of Us-ness, this virtual haven called Oglala Springs. . . .

Oglala Springs Versus the Rest of the Entire Planet: A Map of Two Mutually Exclusive Worlds

The Things from the Left and the Right Columns Cannot Exist Together; If They Come in Contact, They Must Explode

	OGLALA SPRINGS, AKA US (MATTER)	REST OF THE WORLD, AKA THEM (ANTIMATTER)
MOVIE STAR	Meryl Streep	Adam Sandler
TELEVISION PERSONALITY	Charlie Rose	Kathie Lee (obvious)
BRITISH-ACCENTED MOVIE ACTOR	Jeremy Irons	Pierce Brosnan (aka "Jeremy Irons Lite")
THE RICH	Gates	Trump
OFFICE BRIC-A-BRAC	*Morning Edition with Bob Edwards* mug	Golf ball or "NFL Raiders" paperweight
CAR STEREO LISTENING	"Fresh Air" with Terry Gross	Celine Dion singing *Titanic* song or Whitney Houston singing *Bodyguard* song (i.e., you hear that keening cry, "I-I-I will always love you-ou-ou," drifting out of a Toyota minivan and you know you are glimpsing *actual alternate universe*)
OCCUPATION	Assistant professor of French Literature at our wonderful local community college	Commercial real estate, professional golfer
INDIGENOUS SHRUBBERY	Tumbling, unfettered garlands of morning glories, Japanese bansai trees as whimsical and wonderfully eccentric as we are	Any kind of specialized palm tree, e.g., dwarf or royal, such as those found in any of the pink-hued cities (Miami, Palm Springs)—implies this is not a safe space for Us

	OGLALA SPRINGS, AKA US (MATTER)	REST OF THE WORLD, AKA THEM (ANTIMATTER)
COFFEE-TABLE MAGAZINES	*Utne Reader*	*InStyle* magazine *Parade* magazine *Us* (which should really be titled *Them*, to bring out its true Darwinian nature)
MARSALISES	Wynton	Branford (the fact that he took the job band-leading the *Tonight Show*, smiling a lot/ trading quips/kowtowing to the man)

Branford (of course, then Branford *leaves* the *Tonight Show*, decrying it, saying he no longer wants to kowtow to the man) (also, just noticed on NPR website now Branford seems to have his own classic jazz radio show)

Branford (and yet should he have taken the Leno show in the first place?) (is his selling out an unforgivable breach, the thing you can never live down, akin to posing spread-eagle in *Playboy*?) (you know *Wynton* would never have done such a thing)

(continued)

Acceptable Celebrity Vibrations

	OGLALA SPRINGS, AKA US (MATTER)	REST OF THE WORLD, AKA THEM (ANTIMATTER)
JUDDS	Ashley (but only the Ashley of *Ruby in Paradise* or other Miramax-style independents grossing less than $20 million)	Naomi, Wynonna, any possible others
FRANS	Leibowitz	Tarkenton (unsure even why he is a celebrity— my guess is that he is former football player, football coach, or possibly even ex-golfer) (Realtor?)
BEATLE WIVES	(The Reviled) Yoko Ono	(The Late) Linda McCartney (litmus test: "Would a Hallmark Movie of the Week ever be made about this person?" Linda: yes; Yoko: no)
SIBLING MOVIE TEAMS	The Brothers Coen	The Sisters Ephron (i.e., the post–*Harry Met Sally* Meg Ryan* years—what we are talking about is the sanitizing Meg Ryanization of Woody Allen's original formulation of Manhattan [circa era of *Annie Hall*], akin to fabulous yuppie condos with butcher-block counters and Sub-Zero fridges going up on what used to be a brave, tattered, and poetic Upper West Side)

Haunting Question: Roberto Benigni . . . ours or theirs?

*In point of fact, when it comes to the recent feud between my older sister Kaitlin and me (not that she seems remotely aware of it), I think *You've Got Mail* was actually the straw that broke the camel's back.

There are basically two types of families in this world: Families That Support (with cheerful family T-shirts and cheerful family photo collages and cheerful family newsletters) and Families That Judge. Mine would be the latter, and of those members, Kaitlin is the alpha dog, the ringleader, the Supreme Court judge. There is no major life choice I can make that Kaitlin does not deem wrong ("Drop out of grad school? Try to become a novelist? Pursue your dreams? NO!"). There is no minor life choice she'll sign off on, either. Dressing for dinner, pleased with a new purchase, I step out of the bedroom in a fuzzy red turtleneck and purple-and-black striped harem pants. *Without even looking up from her magazine,* Kaitlin throws up one perfectly manicured hand and declares flatly: "NO!"

So—this particular time—I'm visiting Kaitlin up in Marin (her half-million-dollar townhouse: twenty-five hundred square feet, soaring ceilings, miles of bay windows, a benumbing, bewildering maze of sparkling ocean views) (a successful financial consultant, Kaitlin has a stock portfolio that just keeps splitting and splitting and splitting) (even Kaitlin's no-fault divorce has been a rousing, energizing success) . . .

Anyway, I'm up with Kaitlin in Marin and, exhausted from the process of picking over our lives in detail, we hie ourselves out to what *supposedly* promises to be a light little PMS divertissement called *You've Got Mail.* But instead of the relaxation of a gentle estrogen soak, I find myself sitting with clenched fists in a darkened movie theater as I stare, with growing horror, at this Brave New World called New York—a sickeningly sweet carousel of pert, button-nosed blondes, a cloying use of "Rockin' Robin," *the total absence of Jews.* (I myself am not a Jew—of Sino-Germanic descent, I'm a vaguely Latina-looking person of Lutheran upbringing raised in Southern California who has absolutely no cultural identity whatsoever, but I'm telling you, as a fellow outsider to the mainstream, I do recognize something of myself in the Jews.

The Jews are my homeboys, the team I root for, my very own Green Bay Packers [a football team, yes?] on that vast gridiron [right word?] of Life. I am that yellow-fanged codger in too-high houndstooth polyester pants, driving my beat-up eighteen-year-old Honda through the howling, garish Sunset Strip of mass-media culture, shaking my fist out the window and screaming: "Where are the Jews?! See! See! Look how they're getting rid of the Jews!")

Anyway, so at the end of *You've Got Mail*—this moving-picture postcard of a "new, improved" New York *with no one Jewish in it,* this cinematic *holocaust* of a romantic comedy—over the strains of (what else but) "Somewhere Over the Rainbow," I turn in the half-darkness and see that my sister, the self-appointed Judge Judy of the known universe . . . I see, in this eerie *Invasion of the Body Snatchers*/pod-people moment, that Kaitlin loved, loved, loved . . . this movie! Her eyes are literally dewy with tears.

And when Kaitlin and I go to lunch afterward, at some anonymously attractive Bay Area chicken-salad-on-a-baguette place (track lighting like a Nazi interrogation, blond woods swirling nightmarishly all around us, frondy almost-like-a-dwarf palms), I can see that Kaitlin's enthusiasm for *You've Got Mail* is *completely untinged by irony.* Her enthusiasm for the movie is totally unprefaced by "I'm ashamed to say this, but . . ." Or "Call it a guilty pleasure, but . . ." No, she just goes on and on and on—what innocent, escapist fun *You've Got Mail* was, how she loved the oldies music, how she enjoyed the sheer old-fashioned, even nostalgic feel of the story. . . . (And I'm thinking hysterically, Nostalgic? Nostalgic for what? For a time in America when there . . . *were no Jews?*)

And in the months that follow, you just have to say the title of the movie, *You've Got Mail,* and Kaitlin's entire face lights up. You just have to say the words "You've Got Mail!" to Kaitlin and she sits up and beams, as if to say, "Yea! I've got mail!" Do you understand? If I were to say *I* had mail, Kaitlin would flash back judgmentally with, "What—telephone not good enough for you?" but if *Meg Ryan* has mail, somehow, well . . .

Thirty Seconds Later

●

A Knock at My Bedroom Door

●

New Year's Day Crisis

"**N**o, Ben!" I call out. "Forget it! I told you—I'm not up to seeing *anyone* today."

"It's not Ben," a familiar voice says flatly.

"Shit!" I flap out of bed, causing pillows and Kleenex boxes and empty Tupperwares to topple in 360 degrees around me. I dash to the bedroom door, whip a pair of sweatpants off the knob, grab a chair, struggle to angle its back against the—

There is cursing from the other side of the door, wild grinding sounds with the lock; I hear Ben murmuring, "Okay. You just turn it *this* way, then *that* way, then put your leg on it, and *push.* . . ."

The door bursts open.

Exceptionally crisp this morning in Ann Taylor polo shirt and khakis, Kaitlin sweeps in, my betraying husband two steps behind.

"Thanks, Ben," Kaitlin says. She plumps herself down on the bed, plucking a mandala of Kleenexes off the comforter in distaste.

"Ben!" I groan, blowing my nose. "I told you—you have to stop calling my sister every time . . ."

Ben just shakes his head grimly as he moves through the room, parting long-closed curtains, clicking open long-locked windows.

"Thanks," Kaitlin murmurs to him, waving a perfectly manicured hand in front of her face. "It smells like a fart in here."

"It's not a fart—it's turkey," I say icily.

"Turkey?" Kaitlin's eyes widen. Her perfect size-four, effort-lessly-slim-as-a-greyhound body tenses. "Don't tell me you're on another one of your weird crackpot diets?"

"For your information," I say, keeping my voice very, very, very steady as I tuck one last Tupperware under the night table, "it's not a 'weird crackpot diet.' As I've said, it's called the Zone—it's been a *New York Times* bestseller for years now. . . ."

"Oh, please!" Kaitlin exclaims. "Everyone knows the Zone doesn't work! It's based on nothing scientific!"

"If you've flown down here from San Francisco to cheer me up, you're doing a hell of a job!" I lash back. "When I burst into tears, you'll know your work is done!"

Kaitlin gives a reluctant sigh, takes my hands in hers. Her grasp is both comforting but also gluelike; she's like an Ur–Barbara Walters who is going to force you to cry on camera no matter what.

"This is an intervention," Kaitlin announces. "You've been lying around in this bedroom for practically a whole year now. You spend hours and hours doing nothing but reading strange books, eating strange foods, and . . . and . . . what do you call it?"

"Journaling—she calls it journaling," Ben yells out from the corner, where he's stooped over, picking up clothes.

"Journaling," she repeats, curious. "I didn't even know that *was* a verb!" She shakes her head. "Anyway, the point is, you're in a rut. God knows I've done everything *I* can to snap you out of it. I've phoned, I've visited, I've FedExed you a full complement of self-help literature—" She waves a perfectly manicured hand at the tumbledown shantyville of Self-Esteem in the corner. "And *Ben* has tried." She flaps a hand generously in the other direc-tion. "God knows he has tried. Your husband has listened to you, he has supported you, he has *tried* to get you out of town for a vacation who knows *how* many times—"

"A vacation?" I erupt. "Great idea! Spending *tons of money* we don't have from the book advance I'm never going to *get*."

Two pairs of hands fly up, in synch as Rockettes, in a single "Tell it to the hand" motion.

"And then guess what happens this past Christmas holiday?" Kaitlin continues, the enforced sweetness in her voice turning a little sharp. Here it comes. "The family is all gathered there, in Carmel, sitting around that beautiful holiday table—your dad and your stepmom and me and Cousin Stanley and his wife and his teenaged kids and Auntie Ping and Tante Lotte and oh, look! Here's this empty chair! An empty chair! Where you usually sit!"

"I told you all in that letter," I say sulkily. "I've decided to take a personal sabbatical . . . from the family."

"Sabbatical?"

"I told you," I forge on. "This is the year . . . I've been trying to focus all my energy on my novel. And in doing so, I need to eliminate all emotional distractions. Of which our family is Exhibit Number One."

"Uh-huh," she says. "And how's the book going?"

I bite my lip. I feel a hot rush of tears coming.

"Ben says he can't even remember the last time you set foot in that office."

My office. My suffocating broom closet of a home office. It's like that unspeakable back bedroom in *Psycho* where the stuffed dead mother is rocking. My God! The sheer visceral horror of it! The dust, the clutter, the cardboard Christian Brothers Brandy boxes bulging with tattered research Xeroxes and fading limp outlines and DOA pages. I've outlined the second half of that novel one hundred times if I've outlined it once. Behind that poorly framed ranch-style door, the outlines are by now probably gnawing on one another, pages shredding, like weasels.

I close my eyes. The horror, the horror.

"In the meantime," Kaitlin adds, "Ben says you gave one heck of a New Year's party last night."

"Good God, Ben!" Finding a target for the blame, I come to life, throw a pillow at my betrayer. "Is there *anything* you don't tell her? It's like living with a spy!"

Mute as a stone, the husband ducks, then leaves.

"Tell me about last night," Kaitlin murmurs, again taking my hand. "I know it was disappointing for you."

"Well . . ." I hate to give in so easily to her Stalinist/Interventionist agenda.

But then the awfulness of it hits me afresh.

"IT WAS LIKE THE WORST NEW YEAR'S PARTY EVER!" I cry out. "I swear, I'll never throw a New Year's party again, not as long as my savagely celebration-impaired friends live!"

"Tell me about it," she repeats, in a sonorous Marianne Williamson tone.

I list the points on my fingers. "I mean, I get the gravlax from Trader Joe's—"

"Trader Joe's has gravlax?"

One sentence into my story, I am already irritated.

"Okay, maybe not gravlax exactly, but this kind of *gravlaxy stuff* they carry—it's vacuum-packed, with, like, peppercorns. I think it's from Oregon. . . ."

"Go on," she says, suppressing revulsion.

"Anyway," I say, "I go to Trader Joe's and get some sort of *festive holiday poached salmon fish product.* I buy a couple of bottles of Korbel, real Korbel—"

"Korbel is great," she says.

"I get the party hats, I get the horns, I make up these color-coded cards on which to write down our New Year's resolutions—you know, color-coded so you can write down serious, medium, and funny resolutions—and then I've made up this other set of cards so you can write down resolutions for other people, it's this great game I heard about on *Weekend Edition*, supposedly Amy Tan and John Irving do it at their New Year's parties, it's supposed to be really fun, really hilarious, kind of like Scruples, but you know, without a timer—"

"I don't think Scruples has a timer—"

"Anyway! Whatever! The point is, we don't even *make it through* the buffet because of course it turns out Ellis isn't drinking, Jolene's in AA, Ted has a food allergy, something related to seafood, and the gravlax, Bob has to get home by ten because he's convinced that at midnight, when the numbers change, that new AOL virus is going to erase his entire hard drive—"

Kaitlin's brow tenses. "What AOL virus?"

"The one called Dioscorides," I say. "I think it's a character from Dante. Dioscorides. See? At this point, even our AOL *computer viruses* are fifty times more colorful than we are! So Bob takes off, everyone else is tired, they've got the drive home ahead of them, they're scared of getting stuck on the 405 at midnight and getting hit in the head with a falling bullet, from some trailer park or barrio person's celebratory rifle, because after all it is Los Angeles—"

"I think that happened in New Orleans—"

"Whatever! The point is, this is L.A., we have the guns, the danger, the ethnic unrest, the people, they're angry, New Year's Eve in L.A., it's a death sentence. So at a quarter to eleven, a full hour early so everyone can beat the traffic home, we *pretend* it's midnight. We gather in a circle, we link arms, we put on our hats, we sing 'Auld Lang Syne,' and, looking around the room, at all the old familiar faces, it hits me." I stop, dramatic. "I need totally new friends."

"What?" Kaitlin is frowning.

"There's this Gap commercial," I say, feeling this sorrow opening up within me, like a dank, yawning cavern. "You know—the one with the swing-dancers? And they're all in these cute khaki pants, and they're swing-dancing?"

"I love that commercial!" Kaitlin exclaims, her whole body lighting up. (As if to say, "I've Got Mail! I've Got Mail!")

"It makes me . . . physically . . . sick," I declare flatly, popping her Meg Ryan "Up with People" bubble before it swells any further. "Because whenever I see that Gap ad, I can't help thinking those Gap swing-dancers are having more fun in thirty seconds *than I will ever have in my entire life!* They're living life with one thousand times more vigor than me—harder, faster, better, whipping their hair back in laughter—and that laughter, that raucous yawp, is rocking them, it's just rocking them. . . ."

"Swing-dancing is fun," Kaitlin puts in, undaunted. "You should try it."

"Don't you see?" I close my eyes, groan. "Don't you see? My whole life is . . . is *anti*-swing. I live in an *anti*-swing-dance world. Look at the people I'm surrounded with. Look at my pallid, low-fat smorgasbord of thirtysomething friends. They fall into maybe . . . five different categories." I tick these off.

"One, friends who are only available once every three months, for lunch. That's Tuesdays or Thursdays, from precisely twelve-thirty to one-thirty P.M. You have to drive right to their office building on Wilshire and Doheny, page them from the front lobby, wait until they come down to the back door, and then drive the two of you over to the cheesy Mediterranean bistro called Caboodles! nearby, where parking is fourteen dollars and a mess.

"Two, friends who leave loving, elaborate—even tearful—fifteen-minute-long messages on your answering machine once every two years at approximately eleven-oh-five at night . . . *long distance from Paris*, where they now live with the financier they're madly in love with called Jean-Paul. Next time you happen to be *in* Paris, with a few days off, why, you must, must, must call her! You are *such* an important person in her life! Fly yourself right on out to France and she'll *show* you how much she cares.

"Three, friends who have morphed into half of a couple you no longer recognize. They call you twice a year to invite you to barbecues with thirty or more of their coworkers from Xerox in Hermosa Beach for their . . . Super Bowl party, or Kentucky Derby party, or some equally distancing and alienating mass-cultural group activity.

"Four, friends who always urgently want to see you and who always urgently cancel at the last moment for an even *more* urgent reason (child has fever/stomach problems, cat had convulsions, they were up all night in the emergency room, their antidepressant medication had unexpected seesaw effect, etc.).

"Five, friends who, like the Unabomber, have become total hermits. Their communications are restricted to monthly mass e-mailings that do little but reveal what utterly Alien Beings they have become. These include:

"(A) the individual whose entire personality has collapsed into the ritual mass-forwarding of unfunny Top 10 Joke Lists.

"(B) the individual whose entire personality has collapsed into the ritual mass-spewing of dreamy missives advocating strange bands or puppet dance companies or cable shows or infomercial websites no normal human being could possibly be interested in.

"(C) the individual whose entire personality has collapsed into the ritual mass-forwarding of monthly AOL virus warnings. Everything capitalized, prose hysterical: 'If the subject line reads, "GET YOUR FREE MILLION DOLLARS NOW!" and the sender is "HAPPY SUNNY SMILEY FACE," absolutely do not open the attached file! Absolutely do not open!' And you're thinking, Happy Sunny Smiley Face? I no longer bother to open e-mail from friends whose names I *recognize*."

When I open my eyes, I realize I've been sitting alone on my toppled throne, talking to an empty bedroom. Outside the door, I can hear Kaitlin and Ben conferring.

After a beat, the two of them reenter, businesslike and grim as midget nuns in a Fellini movie.

"Sweetie?" Kaitlin asks. "What was the name of that therapist you used to see?"

"Ruth," I croak, collapsing back onto the pillows.

Kaitlin turns to Ben. She no longer even bothers to aim comments in my direction, referring to me in the dreaded third person.

"How often does she see Ruth?" Kaitlin asks.

"Once every four years," Ben replies.

Kaitlin's eyebrows fly up.

"Because she's like three hundred dollars an hour!" I call out weakly. "Which I can hardly afford, with all the money I'm *not* making from the book I should have *finished* by—!"

Kaitlin opens her checkbook, inscribes a check, tears it out. Hands it to Ben.

"You've taken this as far as you can," she murmurs, patting his shoulder. "Now you need to bring in a professional. Send her to Ruth, Ben. Send her to Ruth."

January 10

2:43 p.m.

A Breezy 72 degrees,
a Mystical Wind from the East

Malibu
Something Like
100174 Pacific Coast Highway

●

Therapy Session

($300 an Hour)

●

Ruth

I sit quietly, my hands cupping an orange, slightly nubbly earthenware mug of Yogi tea, amid the pitched ceilings, dangling ferns, and seventies—if immaculately maintained—white shag throw rugs that define Ruth's glamorous shipwreck of a living room. Texturing the walls in sinuous tapestry are windchimes, Tibetan idols, the cawing red and purple and green heads of perpetually laughing and/or screaming animals. To my right, across thirty feet of glass, the Pacific Ocean sprays and crashes.

A cadre of overalled Latino workers are carrying in a small flotilla of antique Balinese masks, the latest additions to the menagerie. Ruth, a massive, statuesque woman of wildly uncertain age—body like an eight-foot-tall Grecian vase, shimmering robin's-egg-blue caftan, loose wavelets of black and gray-streaked hair—directs them.

"No, Manuel," Ruth intones, in her deep, slightly breathy voice. "No. I mean two feet higher. Sí. Sí."

I stare out at the sea. Now that I'm actually here, back in Ruth's presence after four years, I have to admit I'm weirdly excited. Ruth Weingard is like this . . . psychic auto mechanic. She's the Click and Clack of emotional breakdowns. You think your vehicle is totaled, and Ruth merely takes her Phillips No. 3 wrench, unbends a piston (sometimes her advice being as simple as "You need to eat a large sandwich at three in the afternoon") . . . and you're back on the freeway.

24

On a larger scale, Ruth has given me amazing direction in my life.

Twelve years ago, Ruth commanded me to leave Bruce (dreadful Bruce, that rheumy millstone, that blast of clammy, fetid air) and move in with Ben. Who I'm currently not speaking to, but still.

Eight years ago, Ruth commanded me to quit the known path of English graduate school, and Teaching, and set my tentative feet upon the path of Fiscal Indetermination, and Art.

Four years ago, struggling with all my freelance magazine writing jobs, I couldn't decide between rewriting my bad play, rewriting my even more horrible screenplay, or taking a flier on my sketchy idea for a novel. Ruth gave me a powerful, descriptive word for the vague, nagging feeling I was having: *shalampti* (the dreary state, peculiar to all freelance writers, of not knowing which unfunded project to begin next). She commanded me to focus on the novel, and no other thing.

And so, in one extended burst of free-writing, during these magical—even mystical—few weeks in which I can hardly remember eating or sleeping or bathing or breathing, I hacked through. One hundred pages. I believe I was able to so fully immerse myself, to so fully lose myself, because the subject matter was so marvelously removed from my own drear life. In a nutshell, I'd spent the entire summer reading this fascinating, encyclopedic book called *Red Congo*, which detailed the true story of a group of naive British missionaries who'd ventured deep into the Congo to try to build a hospital, practically with their own bare (not to mention woefully under-inoculated) hands. *Red Congo* was the kind of fatalistic page-turner one absolutely could not put down, with its continual, merciless onslaught of philosophically ironic, frighteningly easily avoided tragedies (if anyone had had the foresight to stick just one pair of ordinary aspirin in the medicine kit, *just one pair of ordinary aspirin*) flying at you like swarms of tsetse flies, and you're crying out, "No! No! Oh, no! You guys are not *seriously* going to try to go up the cholera-infested Motaba River in just a . . ." You turn the page, see the ominous title of a brand-new chapter, "Dinghy," gasp sharply, put a hand to your chest, and breathe: "Oh God, no."

So in the middle of reading Red Congo (I think, literally, in the middle of a surprise attack by river eels) (at night!) (isn't that great? a river eel–attack . . . at night!) this lightbulb goes off over my head. My idea: What if an idealistic American woman missionary ventured into the Congo, during the same slightly antiquated era, on a similarly impossible mission? Here was a naive young female, an avid reader (like me) who'd read far too many books about the Congo—and not cautionary and scientific accounts like Red Congo, but the vastly more romanticized books of her time, novels of the early 1900s that depicted the archetypal journey to the Congo as some kind of noble and uplifting adventure. I could intersperse passages about the real Congo with passages from novels she was reading about a fictional Congo. Here would be the tragedy of an overprotected young woman's unrealistic expectations, and the subtle arrogance of the Western intellectual mind.

And, well, something must have clicked, because those fateful one hundred pages turned out to be good enough to actually win a literary award. And not just any award—the prestigious Winkler Prize for First Fiction, given out annually by the Goodman Foundation for the best one hundred pages of an unfinished first novel (I think Jane Smiley got one) (or Jayne Anne Phillips?) (one of the Janes). The take included a thousand dollars and a first-look commitment from Winkler Press (a brand-new imprint of Penguin/Putnam/Berkley). The very next day after learning that I'd won the award, I received a congratulatory fax from the offices of the Georges Borchardt Agency (Samuel Beckett/Grove Press/ etc.). "When you finish the novel . . ." it said, speaking quietly, and confidently, of the future.

I stared at this amazing fax, and for the first time in my adult life—a tangled, rudderless snarl of botched opportunities, half-finished graduate degrees, countless odd mini-careers attempted and quickly abandoned (including even, for a short time, a one-woman cabaret act—the less said about that the better) . . . Anyway, I stared at this fax and realized that I had finally, somehow, in some way, thanks to some angel above, stumbled onto my life's work. At long last, here was a task upon which I could bend the chaos of my perennially scattered attentions. Here was something that offered a sense of purpose that would transport me from the dusty flatlands of life to a clean mountain high road far less traveled, far less easy, and hence far more worthwhile. What was I? I was a novelist. My mission? Finish the book.

The fax is still tacked to my bulletin board in the *Psycho* home office, behind a locked door, yellowing.

"Sandra?" Ruth says, settling next to me, in a cloud of Lagerfeld. "How are you?"

"I've been blocked on my novel for three straight years," I admit. That's the thing: When your family's paying three hundred dollars an hour for therapy, you don't pussyfoot around.

"A Block," Ruth repeats thoughtfully. She leans back in her Hopi-print armchair, putting the tips of her beringed fingers together. "Creative Blocks are marvelously complex things that have their own unique geometries." Ruth fixes her eyes on a far-distant object. Her voice is gently, infinitely patient. "So Sandra, dear heart, can you tell me . . . What is the shape of this Block?"

"Shape?"

"Is your Block sort of a continuous, buzzing, *flat* thing, like an ever-present white noise, or hum? . . . You hear that?" She looks up suddenly, jabbing a finger toward the ceiling. "Hear that hum?"

"Yes," I admit. "Now that you mention it, I do."

"It's the damn central air," Ruth says. "The workmen put in a new pump for the koi pond last week and it seems to have affected—Anyway!" she says abruptly. "Is your Block like a continual sort of buzzy *flat* thing, what I like to call electrical in nature, or is it more solid, like a one-hundred-ton glacier?"

"Glacier," I answer immediately. "With tiny, electric-blue cracks of despair in it. That every so often leak these sort of . . . spidery, hairline tears."

"Aha!" she exclaims, eyes widening. "Spidery tears! I *like* that." She pats my hand, beams, proffers a small plate of snap beans. I take a couple, feeling thrilled. This is what I love about

Ruth. She understands how, sometimes, the most creative thing about a Writer can *be* her Block. "Now we're getting somewhere! And Sandra, dear heart, these spidery tears . . . Let's say sometimes they slo-o-owly leak, and sometimes they freeze up a little, and ache, and maybe give you a little shock—"

"Yes!" I murmur, getting her gist. "Icy stabs! Icy stabs!"

"Icy stabs," she repeats. "Hmm. Tell me where you are when such an Icy Stab might come. Tell me what is happening."

"Okay," I say. "I am . . ."

I falter. Nothing is coming to me. Even when it comes to narratives involving my own *Writer's Block*, I draw a blank.

"Tunnel deeper," she says huskily. "To maybe a . . . maybe a darker place."

Darkness. Night. I close my eyes. A scene pops to me.

"Cahuenga Boulevard," I mutter, trancelike. "Hollywood. Ten o'clock at night. Cue the helicopters wheeling overhead . . ."

Cahuenga Boulevard? Helicopters? This is the first fresh narrative idea I've had in years! I'm excited. This is *way* off the standard menu of stories I tell about myself. I truly have no idea where I'm going with this.

"Go on," she says.

"Okay," I continue, concentrating on each image. "I see myself walking. Alone. Glamorously alone. I pass a . . . a . . . a newsstand. Rows and rows of glossy magazines glimmer under the street lamps like toxic jewels. And I feel this kind of . . . this kind of choking feeling coming on."

"The locus of the pain," she breathes. "We're getting closer. Where's the center of it? Where's the center?"

But now I'm feeling literal horror because in this vision the ghost Me now shoots a furtive look over her shoulder and picks up . . . "The new *Vanity Fair* featuring Nicole Kidman on the cover—*This isn't right!*" I break off suddenly. *"This isn't what I'm doing!"*

"Who are you to say what dark things live in your subconscious?" Ruth admonishes sternly. "Keep tunneling to the core! Keep tunneling!"

"I *open* the *Vanity Fair*," I continue, with growing horror.

"And once again, that familiar conga line of glamorous people in Armani tuxes and little black cocktail dresses and the fabulous hair, you know, the hair that is always fabulously swinging outwards—" What am I *babbling* about? I think to myself, helplessly.

"Swingy hair?" Ruth queries, calmly picking out a few more snap beans. "What do you mean, swingy hair?"

"Swingy hair!" my Id shrieks, and like a ghastly homunculus, it now breaks fully out of its beastie-box, skittering about tangle-limbed in broad daylight. "Like in a perfume ad—by Bijan! Although in a way he was very eighties! But that's what Swingy Hair signifies: that Bijan moment, that moment of sheer, barking, tear-your-head-off joy! The moment where a heart-stoppingly gorgeous woman (who is six feet tall!) is so excited, so amazed, so *electrified* by this hot *new* flavor of perfume, shampoo, lipstick . . ." My voice is a bird-screech. "Like Revlon Red! My God! Revlon Red is never less than an explosion—a supernova—of color! One look and these heart-stoppingly gorgeous *Vanity Fair*/Helmut Newton/Revlon Red women (who as I've said are always six feet tall, I mean they are Amazons! dirigibles! they've been rocket-shipped to the photo shoot from Venus!) . . . I mean, one look at Revlon Red and a one-hundred-piece band *must* break into trumpet calls and a thousand ten-foot-tall blond women *must* break out of a million cycloramas in gold lamé pants! While of course the hair swings out! In unison! One thousand heads of fantastic hair, pitching back in ecstatic laughter, the metallic tsunami of brilliance, the joyous yawp!"

The crazed minotaur that used to be me takes a great gulping breath of oxygen and falls back, exhausted by the tidal wave, Bijan, the yawp, the hair.

Ruth is looking sad for me, very sad.

"Or like in the Gap ad," my Ugly Head adds. "You know the one where—"

"They're swing-dancing in the khaki pants," Ruth says. "Yes. A lot of my manic-depressives have problems with that Gap ad. But keep going. What about the Icy Stabs?"

"The Icy Stabs . . ." And well, why *shouldn't* I keep going? The session is a disaster anyway. It is not helping, it is not healing, it is not inspirational. Quite the opposite. Indeed, as I spiral lower into the proverbial tunnel, I feel my words becoming literally smaller, my thoughts super-tiny, unworthy, like ants.

"I turn the page and I see it—the fabulous photo of some writer ten years younger than me with fabulous hair getting, like, a three-hundred-thousand-dollar advance on their first novel. At a Manhattan cocktail party with Morgan Entrekin and . . . and Binky."

I'm totally mumbling now, humiliated at having the vast mystical architecture of my creative Block exposed, finally, as something so pathetic, so petty, so mundane.

"Well, that's how I feel, at age thirty-five. Have you ever seen that bumper sticker that says, 'Just when you think you won the rat race, along come faster rats'?"

"So you get Icy Stabs when you see reminders that (a) you're not famous and (b) you're old?" Ruth asks, with uncharacteristic bluntness.

"I mean, I hate to reduce it to that!" I protest, stung. "There are many other complex factors at work, you know!" Isn't Denial one of the early stages of Kübler-Ross? God. My psyche should be in a medical textbook. "But yes, yes . . ." And in one last hiss of dragon-steam, the awful truth finally blorts out. "I will admit, at the basest level, I *am* jealous of the celebrity of others. Late at night, I click into *Politically Incorrect with Bill Maher* and I scream! The guests are Ted Danson, Bella Abzug, Magic Johnson, and *my ex–college roommate Cindy*, dumb as a brick, who has suddenly become like this well-loved sports commentator on ESPN 2, who apparently everyone loves, and Cindy's getting off these witty zingers and the whole audience is roaring with laughter and Bill Maher is totally fascinated. 'Well!' he erupts. 'You've certainly told us!'

"I mean, why should I even finish my novel? I'll make no difference in this world. In the vast media wash, I am nothing. Not that that's ever been my goal—in fact, that's one of the things I least respect about America. Our marginalization of the Artist!" I wobble on, throwing some last-minute pomposity onto my list of unappealing personality traits. "Do you know the career seesaws Branford Marsalis has been through? Have you been following that? All that stuff with Branford Marsalis?"

With one movement, Ruth stills the waving crab claws that

used to be my hands. With a grim nod of her head, she signals for me to continue.

"I shouldn't feel like an utter human zero, but I do. Why? Because I am not a well-loved female sports commentator on ESPN 2. I'm not the eleventh guy from the left in the bar of *Cheers.* I'm not some lovable Man on the Street in a funny FedEx ad. *The View!*" I careen suddenly sideways. "The women on *The View!* What is *that* show about? Why are those women *on* there? Lisa Ling? What are *her* credits? And now why is she in these Old Navy commercials? Dancing, dancing, dancing with those pants? And the swingy hair?" This has become less of a therapy session and more of a *colonic purging*—all one can do is look on from the sidelines and wanly remark, "Look at that . . . corn." My mouth widens, Roman mask–like, into a bitter howl. "Why why why not me me me me me me me me me?"

I run out of language. The only sounds you can hear are the groan/crash of the Pacific, and the faint sound of hammering from some distant piazza in Ruth's redwood manse. Ruth is standing before the plate glass of the Pacific, looking out at the slate-gray waves.

"Sandra, dear heart," Ruth says, finally, turning. "Listen very carefully. I see you . . ." She narrows her eyes, continues to speak as though in a dream. "I see you as a toad in a cave, looking out a hole, watching the world outside. But in fact you are looking into a pond, and the hole is a reflection, of something inside . . . *what you think is* the cave. Do you follow me?" I don't, but I feel far too exposed in my splattered Thought Vomitorium to say so.

"You need to light the bier," she says, "to create the burning, whose force will open . . . the flue. Because while crouching down low, to stare into the pond, you looked for a place to sit down, and in so doing, you've moved the boulder, on top of the match. (And in the meantime, I think because of the Mind Attic Clutter, you seem to be confusing *lodestone* with the idea of *marrow.* You need to realize that energy is all around you! Energy is all around you! But in tiny nano-particles.)"

I stare at her, slack-jawed.

"Cave paintings," she insists. "Make peace with the cave paintings! Which they aren't really, of course, because it's not truly a cave." She shrugs, waves a turquoise-and-silver hand, dismissive. "It's just wallpaper."

I am lost. The trouble with Ruth is that, at heart, she thinks only in terms of home furnishings. If only she could translate this Malibu language into something a little more Van Nuys.

"So . . ." I say. "If I figure out that . . . metaphor, will that unblock me?"

"I'm going to give you something that's going to set you on a journey," she announces.

Oh no, I'm thinking. Not another amulet, another I Ching coin, another brand of herbal tea.

I look down into her extended hand. It contains a slip of paper.

"This is the number of a client of mine," Ruth says. "A guest booker from *Donny and Marie*. Wait one week, then call her. And trust in the process."

"A booker?" I recoil from the paper. "From *Donny and Marie*?"

"Yes," Ruth murmurs. "It's your labyrinth, and you must walk it. And when you get to the end . . ."

"What?" I ask. "What?"

But the hour's up.

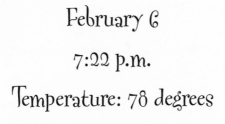

February 6

7:22 p.m.

Temperature: 78 degrees

Van Nuys

While Ben stir-fries,

I attack him with my amazing news. . . .

•

Political Pundit

"Well . . . what is it?" Ben asks warily, looking up from a sizzling wok.

"My amazing news is . . ." I announce, barely able to contain my amazement. "I've been asked to appear on CNN!"

"You—on CNN?" Ben's chopsticks freeze in midair. His eyes widen.

"I mean, I'd *thought* this woman was a booker for *Donny and Marie*," I jabber on. "Ruth gave me her number, she's a Ruth client, it's all somehow part of my path, or my labyrinth, to use the more specific word. . . . But it turns out this woman just moved over from *Donny and Marie* to CNN, which is a million times better because Charlie Rose is much more serious, and besides, as you know, being on Charlie Rose has always been kind of a secret dream of mine. Not that Charlie Rose is on CNN. I think he's on PBS. But you see how *this* respectable cable thing could lead to that *other* respectable cable thing. . . ." I can see I'm losing Ben in detail. I rush to the conclusion: "Anyway, the point is, they've invited me to be a panelist on the political commentary show *CNN and Company*!"

"You—on CNN?" Ben repeats. And now I realize his shell-shocked expression is less one of surprise than of fear.

Which gives me pause, serious pause.

Understand that, as Kaitlin is the Demon of Judgment in my life, my husband has always been the Angel of Support. Support, Support, Support. Support of one's thoughts. Support of one's plans. Support to a dogged, outrageous, flamboyant degree—indeed, an ex-girlfriend once tagged Ben's agreeability as less *actual* Support than a wild passion for nonconfrontation.

And I'll admit that, twelve years into the relationship, sure, I'm not *totally* unaware that I'm in Denial about my true abilities probably a third of the time, and that my husband, sequestered on the homefront—at Ground Zero of Denial, if you will—is the coconspirator most often called upon to co-Deny. But nor do I think anything's wrong with that. I think a Reality Check Error Factor of about 30 percent is a gift truly loving spouses give each other.

But now, for actual *skepticism* to poke through that reassuring veil of Denial . . .

Good God. This must be really bad. Is there yet some *new* ghastly truth I need to learn about myself? Shallow, I've just learned I am . . . but stupid?

"Well, why *not* CNN?" I ask, trying to mask how stung I feel. "I've been a working journalist for years. I won a prestigious literary prize for my . . . novel-in-progress about the Congo—"

"It's just . . ." Ben shakes his head, scoops up a pile of ginger, drops it into the wok.

"What?" I come over to him, stroke the side of his arm. I soften my voice. "You can tell me." Unfortunately, the illusion of Open Communication is one of those Yalta Conference points of the modern marriage.

Ben speaks carefully as he stirs.

"You are a wonderfully gifted, imaginative person. At the same time, taking nothing away from that, it's also fair to say that politics . . . is not your strongest area."

My voice is also very, very careful. "What do you mean politics is not my strongest area?"

"I seem to recall this dinner party *not* that many years ago where a certain someone broke into tears in the middle of an argument and famously wailed, 'Why do they always fight in the Middle East—isn't it just a bunch of little prefab houses?' "

"Fair enough," I admit, smartly. "But in that case I'd had one too many Bartles and Jameses—see how long ago that was?" I feel smug as a lawyer on Court TV. "I was responsible that night for neither my political views nor the thing about my falling backwards over the dog. Besides," I continue, gathering a head of debating steam, "I've been studying CNN and MSNBC very closely this week! I've scoped out the game, the rhythm, the beat, the look—"

"The look?"

"That's right. Tweed blazer? Small button earrings?" I close my eyes, nod. "I own them."

"You do? I've never seen you in anything but harem pants and a lint-covered T-shirt."

In triumph, I reach over the kitchen chair and pull up my trusty old (if newly dry-cleaned) faux-tweed jacket from my many years as an office temp.

"Ross for Less!" I declare. "Why shop anywhere else? In the old days, yes, perhaps I was a bit more confused, a bit more scattered, a bit more unkempt. By contrast, the new, improved me is a very considered, very intelligent, very measured person. On the preinterview with the CNN person, where we discussed the political landscape? I flew through it! Even the booker applauded me."

"You flew through your interview with the CNN person?" Now Ben is looking scared, actually scared.

"Well, it wasn't so much an *interview* as a *conversation*," I allow. "But that's what a panel show is."

"It is?"

"It is. Because, as I've learned, from careful study, that's the secret to all these political panel shows. No one ever gets more than two sentences in a row out before the next person jumps on them. Everyone keeps interrupting each other, usually yelling. To have an actual point would be a disadvantage. No, all you have to do to seem smart is offer the occasional Transitional Comment."

"I'm lost," Ben says, putting a lid over the wok.

I knew he would be.

I explain: "The Transitional Comment *sounds* like an opinion, but is actually just a conundrum open to interpretation . . . by the next person. Get it? You pass the baton. Pass the baton."

"What?" Ben looks unhappy.

"All right," I say. "Here are some examples . . . to be recited either very dramatically or very quietly, with a wry, knowing laugh."

I clear my throat.

"THE FLAT TAX," I say . . . and then smile, pityingly. "REALLY NOT ALL THAT *FLAT*, IS IT?"

Ben—a monumental reader who ingests *The New York Times* in the bathroom for an hour every morning before turning to *The Atlantic Monthly* as a soothing chaser—gives a bark of laughter, incredulous. A host of objections burst out of him. "Well, of course it—! I mean, that's why Alan Greenspan—! In the thirty-three-percent tax bracket—!"

But then the doubts begin to form. You can see the sheer amount of information Ben knows is beginning to implode on him. There are too many ways to go on the issue, too many arguments, too many angles.

"It's just that, according to Steve Forbes's calculations, not that those are one hundred percent accurate—" His spluttering is slowing down. His electrical circuits are fritzing out. He puts his head into his hands, goes into a glazed mid-focus stare.

"Look at me," I purr, "I'm not even breaking into a sweat. Here's another. BOB DOLE." I shake my head, give a low whistle. "GEEZ."

Ben stares at me. He has no rebuttal—how can he?

"You want a little foreign policy?" I continue. "Listen to this one." I pause, suddenly lean in for effect. "THOSE *RUSSIANS* ARE SURE HAVING A WILD TIME OF IT!"

Ben lets out a groan. "That's absurd. What do you even mean by that? I'll bet *you* don't even know what you mean!"

"Of course I don't! But why do I have to mean anything? You know the Soviets are always up to *something* crazy, what with the seesawing economy, and the wall coming down—"

"That's Berlin," Ben corrects . . . but abstractedly. His brow is furrowed. You can see his mind is still lost and ricocheting in the mirror-halled intricacies of the flat tax.

"All right," I say breezily, "but Russia, Berlin, the Balkans, they're all connected, they've all had hard times, now they're getting the euro, discos are opening, they're wearing the Madonna T-shirts, they're doin' the macarena, it's crazy, it's all bound to cause upheaval somewhere in the . . . in the societal *fabric.* All of which goes to show just one thing."

I pause, lean in.

"What?" An exhausted face turns to me.

"IT'S A MISTAKE TO . . . TO PUT ALL OUR EGGS INTO THE YELTSIN BASKET."

Ben bursts into laughter. He doubles over with it. I calmly wait.

"See, you almost had me going," Ben says, wiping tears from his eyes. *"Almost.* But the one you just said doesn't even *sound* right."

"Well, for your information," I tell him, "that was the one statement I *didn't* make up. That is a verbatim quote from former President of the United States Gerald Ford."

Ben stands absolutely still.

"Gerald Ford," Ben says, "it's true. Still, your giving political insights on CNN. I can't help thinking it's one of the Four Signs of the Apocalypse."

· · · ·

Having survived this unexpected trial by friendly fire, I find myself feeling *even more* confident the night before the taping.

However, I do quail a bit when Jan the booker informs me that I am scheduled to face, on my first nationally televised panel debate show, Republican Congresswoman Susan Molinari and, um, *Newsweek* political analyst Eleanor Clift.

"I'm kind of a *fiction* writer?" I say to Jan. "My novel about the Congo . . . While I've done extensive research, yes, the Congo in my book is less a discrete political entity than a . . . a metaphor for tragic futility, and Western intellectual arrogance. What I mean is, while I'm very much looking forward to the show, are you sure this particular grouping . . . ?"

"Oh no," she tells me. "That's exactly why we want you in the mix! A fresh face!"

A fresh face! That cinches it. Because obviously, when it comes to politics, a lint-covered bohemian such as myself does have a certain freshness. You know? Who can claim to be orbiting farther outside the Beltway than yours truly? Clift and Molinari are experts, yes, but they are nothing—they are business as usual, ho-hum television—without that third, cut-through-the-red-tape, "rubber to the road" *Perot*-type person.

Eight A.M. comes a bit early, but I manage to crawl to the studio in reasonably good form, coffee-ed, showered, and coiffed. (The lint brush has been taken to the Ross for Less jacket, wire-rimmed glasses donned to suggest Competence.)

The *CNN and Company* technician seats me on a chair in front of a camera, gives me an earpiece, clips on a microphone. In a monitor to my right, I can see Mary Tillotsen, our curly-haired, natty-suited host from Atlanta, looking every inch the (idea for a fragrance) CNN Woman.

"Good morning!" Mary says. "Glad to have you with us!"

"My pleasure!" I enthuse.

Mary's image fades and three columns pop onto the screen. On the right, Republican Congresswoman Susan Molinari (New York), Statue of Liberty behind her. In the middle, *Newsweek*'s Eleanor Clift (Washington), Capitol Building behind her. On the left, me, Ms. Fresh Face, smiling just a bit too wildly . . . in front of the eye-gougingly bright pink neon letters of the "Hollywood" sign.

The "Hollywood" sign—this gives me pause.

But before I can fully process this, the red digital clock clicks eight-thirty, the logo—"CNN and Company!"—explodes across the screen, and flying right at us comes Mary Tillotsen herself, talking very quickly in these aggressive verbal bullets: "MINIMUM-WAGE BILL!" "YELTSIN'S REELECTION!" "KAT-YUSKA ROCKETS!"

Clift and Molinari seem to know exactly what Mary Tillotsen is talking about. It's like they can't *wait* for her to bring these canker sores of political infamy up. Honed from their many *MacNeil-Lehrer Newshour*s, they fly at each other like attack dogs about Dole's record on minority whip veto bills regarding tax-free incentives without the crucial 13 percent bipartisan minimum-wage legislation.

I sit quietly, grinning like a hyena, under my pink "Hollywood" sign. As if in slow motion, the clock clicks over to 8:32.

Feeling a void of energy from my box, our host seizes on me for the next issue.

"Sandra?" Mary Tillotsen says. "What do you think about—"

And God bless this woman, what follows is perhaps the most complicated question that's ever been asked in the history of man. Even to utter this question aloud, in English, would kill most people.

All I can tell you about Mary Tillotsen's question is that it begins in Bosnia-Herzegovina, picks up a few Serbs, drops off a few Croats, sideswipes a few Katyuska rockets and B-12 bombers (or is it B-2 bombers? isn't B-12 a kind of vitamin shot?). . . . Anyway, it loops painstakingly over to Afghanistan, darts dizzyingly back in time for a moment to the foreign policy of Richard M. Nixon, corkscrews suddenly, diagonally, to Clinton—not Bill but Hillary—summarily dismisses Gore, just in case you were to bring him up, and lands, if memory recalls, which I admit it doesn't, very well, smack on top of the currency of . . . Brazil. The recent fall of. Or fall of U.S. currency in relation to. The point is, something fell.

An eternity later, Mary Tillotsen finishes this, the unanswerable question. From their boxes, out of the corner of my eye, I can see that Clift and Molinari are dying to answer, but in deference to their esteemed colleague Charo, they're holding their tongues.

I say nothing. My mouth is so dry I can feel sand caking in it.

"Well, Sandra?" Mary Tillotsen prompts. "Would Clinton be wise to launch these rockets, or no?"

"Well, Mary," I say, clearly beaten, my voice wobbling, "I . . . find . . . it . . . difficult . . . to . . . say."

Mary Tillotsen blinks, ponders this a moment, and says, "We'll be right back . . . after the break."

The break comes, and flop sweat begins literally pouring off me. I'm being humiliated on national television, in real time, which seems to keep moving slower and slower and slower.

I now realize that I am not Perot. No, who I'm channeling is his running mate, *Admiral Stockdale.* . . . I envision myself rising and drifting, bemused and lost, out of my third of the screen. Or perhaps I should simply stay in my box and make myself comfortable. As Clift and Molinari continue to argue ("HEZBOL-LAH!" "BOSNIA-HERZEGOVINA!"), Ms. Hollywood could be shown wanly accepting an umbrella drink from the bottom half of a Chippendales dancer, filing her nails, ordering snacks.

But suddenly it comes to me—the bohemian who has always been mocked, abused, and, frankly, befuddled when it comes to anything political, or important. (Bring patriotic music up.)

I am very stupid, yes, I think. Yes I am. Very stupid. But I have met, in this great land, people who are *just as stupid as I am.* The Forrest Gump people. The people who drink too many wine coolers, who are bewildered by the Middle East, the people who . . . who fall over the dog! Who will speak for them today? Who will speak for them? Do we not deserve a voice, too? *Rubber to the road!*

Exploding from the break, I snap out of my trance, jump into the fray. While Clift and Molinari continue yelling at each other, I yell from my box, straight out at the camera. "BOB DOLE—GEEZ!" I exhort. "THE RUSSIANS—THEY'RE SURE HAVING A WILD TIME OF IT!" And finally Mary Tillotsen asks me one more of her fekakta, impossible-to-understand-by-any-real-red-blooded-American questions. The only words I recognize are "the Middle East" and "why."

But in this case, simplicity is a virtue. It gives me focus. This time I speak passionately from the heart—from my *CNN and Company* experience itself.

"It's just—the issues you raise, Mary, the current difficult situation and the rabid fighting . . ." I blurt out. "It's all *just so hard to follow!*" My voice rises in hysteria. I let the energy of it sweep me forward. "It just all seems . . . to go on and on and on. I'm exhausted!" My eyes flick left and I notice the digital red clock reads just 8:47—all this and we're barely halfway through the broadcast! I exhale, at my wit's very end. "Will . . . the . . . horror . . . never . . . end?"

"And you know what?" I tell Ben, on the studio phone, right after the taping. "My friend's old Jewish dad Morrie just called the station and said I was right about Israel. He watched the show from his retirement home. He says when it comes to the Middle East, he's really, really tired, too."

"I'm glad you held your own, sweetie," Ben replies. "But in the future—"

"Sandra?" Jan the booker calls out to me, from the hallway.

She's holding up a phone receiver. It casts a long shadow.

"It's for you! A producer. *From New York.*"

March 6

1:07 p.m.

Temperature: 85 degrees

Van Nuys, Home Office

●

Letter from My New Best Friend

●

Contents:
1 Internet Message Header
2 <no topic> *Binary*
==================== Begin Part 1 ====================
Topic: Internet Message Header
Format: LATIN-1

Sender: abanning@amelia.com
Received: from chewbacca (therep.dsl.speakeasy.net [216.231.46.110])
     for <Sandra46@aol.com>; Mon, 6 Mar 10:47:10 -0800
Reply-To: <abanning@amelia.com>
From: <abanning@amelia.com>
To: <Sandra46@aol.com>
Subject: Writing for Amelia
Date: Mon, 6 Mar 10:50:48 -0800
Message-ID: <0101bf3b63$d1118290$be1514ac@chewbacca.
    womezone.org>
Content-Type: multipart/mixed;
    boundary="----=_NextPart_000_0011_01BF3B20.C2EE4290"
X-Mailer: Microsoft Outlook 8.5, Build 4.71.2173.0
X-MimeOLE: Produced By Microsoft MimeOLE V4.72.3110.3

Dear Sandra,

Denise Francis, our media buyer, says she called you and spoke
with you after your recent appearance on CNN. (She was given a
head's-up about the booking by your therapist, Ruth Weingard,
who happens to be an old friend of hers.) Denise loved your hip,
irreverent take on the world, and suggested we contact you
about the possibility of contributing to Amelia.com, the new
online magazine for women.

    Amelia.com promises to be much more than a website. Our
financing comes from the German conglomerate BFG Worldwide
(a Rupert Murdoch company), who has asked us to be extremely
aggressive as far as growth. Plans for Amelia include a spin-off
magazine and a cable station (an all-Amelia talk show is currently
in development for Oxygen). As such, BFG is extremely interested

in developing Amelia.com's contributors not just as writers but as on-screen/camera-ready "personalities." (You may have seen our health and fitness columnist Randi Duzinger in her recent appearances on *Good Morning America, Later Today,* and *The View.*)

I invite you to visit the working prototype of our website, whose official launch will be next month. In particular, please have a look at the various neighborhoods-in-progress under the pink and red (move cursor left, click twice) Ameliazone banner, i.e.:

BodyZone
ExerZone
HealthZone
FunnyZone

We're interested in short personal essays that could fit into these specific areas.

If you're interested in contributing, please send us a bio and some clips. Thanks!

Anita Banning

Senior Content Editor, Amelia.com

Sender: Sandra46@aol.com
Received: from imo24.mx.aol.com (imo24.mx.aol.com [152.163.225.68])
    by spdmgaac.compuserve.com (8.9.3/8.9.3/SUN-1.7) with
    ESMTP id PAA04465 for <abanning@amelia.com>;
    Fri, 10 Mar 15:14:27 -0500 (EST)
Message-ID:<0.8ed03f7c.2572e71d@aol.com>
Date: Fri, 10 Mar 15:14:21 EST
Subject: Writing for Amelia.com
To: abanning@amelia.com
MIME-Version: 1.0
Content-Type: text/plain; charset="us-ascii"
X-Mailer: AOL 4.0 for Mac - Post-GM sub 54

Dear Anita,

Thanks for your note! I am indeed EXTREMELY interested in writing
for Amelia.com.

~~I confess I've been having MAJOR Writer's Block for the past
THREE years—marooned horribly on a possibly too-ambitious novel
project, my income a miasma of sporadic, desperate bouts of part-
time teaching.~~

Careful study of the Amelia.com website ~~however~~ has trig-
gered a fury of excitement. I ~~actually unlocked my own office and~~
have been writing for three straight days! The result is three short
essays, which I hope you will enjoy.

Aside from my recent appearance on CNN, I've written for
Cosmopolitan, The Los Angeles Times (both Southern California
"Living" and Real Estate sections), *The LA Weekly,* and *The Tolucan.*
I also have clips from the late *Buzz* magazine, the late *EGG* magazine, the late *rebelle* magazine, the late *L.A. SCENE* magazine, the
late *L.A. FLASH* magazine, *HeadCandy* (out of San Francisco), and
also *Married Woman* (one issue, but I believe it was indeed a
Fairchild Publication). My novel-in-progress, *Dreaming of the Congo,*
won the prestigious Winkler Prize for First Fiction and is scheduled
to be published at some future date by the Winkler Press (a brand-
new imprint of Putnam/Penguin/Berkley).

1. Anita, at the beginning of the year, people's thoughts turn toward self-improvement (i.e., How many of us are trying to hang on to those New Year's resolutions we made in January!) (And how many of us are thinking ahead to summer, swimsuit season being just a few agonizing months away?).

What could be more perfect for the BodyZone than an article about a new fad diet?

The Zone Diet

....

g'm on Week 17 of the Zone diet and it's all I want to talk about. My diet. What I *can* eat, what I *can't* eat, the good protein, the bad protein, the weighing of food, the banning of bread, my battles with nonfat cottage cheese, how sometimes I cry in the morning when I face the cottage cheese—the interesting *mix-ins* I'm developing for cottage cheese—avocado, peanut butter, sesame seeds, grapes, tuna, hamburger—and of course, at the end of the day, there is always turkey, turkey, turkey. . . .

"Oh, please," my ~~older sister Kaitlin~~ office colleague Maribeth scoffs. "Everyone knows the Zone doesn't work. It's based on nothing scientific. You're always just better off to eat healthy—but light—and get some regular exercise . . ."

(Author note: I am a person who can do forty-five minutes on the treadmill five days a week, thirty-five minutes of that *running*, eat two low-fat meals a day, and still weigh in the 150s. I'm tallish, but still. You hope for a little more in this sorry life.)

"Have you even *read The Zone?*" I ask, in my iciest tone.

"No, but I've read all the articles that say it's bunk."

"Well," I suggest to my naturally lean *older* ~~sister~~ officemate, the one who everyone always thinks is *younger*. (Why? "It's just—she's so much *tinier* than you," an unthinking male once said.)

"*Well,*" I suggest to my ~~big sister Kaitlin~~ officemate Maribeth, "maybe you should read the book *yourself* before we continue this discussion."

"Well, maybe you should read the articles critiquing it—"

"Well, okay then!"

"Well, okay!"

Later that day, a thought suddenly occurs to me. Where *do* all the articles dissing new diets appear? And how come naturally thin people can always quote them? Is there a kind of secret underground . . . *Thin Person's Magazine*? How come the very people who've never gone on a diet are always the biggest *experts* on the diet field? Where do they get all this wonderful knowledge?

The answer? Nowhere. The fact is, thin people don't . . . know . . . anything. And it's time that we as a culture finally faced this. We've been humoring thin people for too many years, with their purely guesswork, no-basis-in-reality, "Just eat sensibly, take a few walks" patois. We've been sharing our fat, colorful world with them, and frankly, they have no place in it.

The fact is we, the people who are always on diets, are a fascinating, rich, *complex* people. Our bodies combine fats, proteins, and lipids in geometries and algebras thin people can't even imagine. We are the people who can go on the Pill and gain eleven pounds in ten days. Or we can add turkey, cut out toast, and drop fifteen. We can go to New York, consume tons of vodka and pâté, and become thin. We can come back, eat little starvation girlie meals of bran cereal with half a banana for breakfast, low-fat yogurt and fruit for lunch, salad with just a little pasta primavera for dinner, and become fatter and fatter and fatter.

We are the Jenny Craig people, who have known the abject, Joseph Conradian "Heart of Darkness" terror of staring at a single bagel chip at seven in the evening and knowing this is all that stands between us and bed. We are the Dr. Atkins Diet people, deliriously awash in tuna and olive oil and the light hallucinations of ketosis. And of course, armed with curry powder, soy sauce, nonfat mayonnaise, and Tabasco, we have done more with popcorn than should be legal.

We have been places you'll never know.

In short, you naturally lean *experts* out there, why don't *you* go for a walk? And . . . pass the turkey.

2. Anita, I found the ExerZone area extremely useful, and illuminating (especially the pieces on Tae-Bo, pregnancy aerobics, and ribbon-dancing). While I myself can claim little personal experience in the field of exercise, I do belong to a gym. And, let's face it, while on the one hand, health club membership is a growing phenomenon in this busy age of the working woman, on the other, given the urban sprawl that we are all increasingly becoming used to, whether we're aware of it or not, I'm sure many of your target audience members, like me, find themselves through geographic circumstances unable to attend the #1 health club of their choice. ~~This sentence and in fact whole concept is a mess but will have to leave as is for now.~~

I think the following piece would be a splashy, irreverent entry in the ExerZone.

Bargain Health Club

• •

*J*ust between the two of us. No one's listening. Lean in.
I am one. Are you? Are you a member of a "Bargain Health Club," too?

If so, let us unite in fellowship, laughter, even triumph. Let us not think of ourselves as hapless losers in gross T-shirts driving bad cars. Let us not feel sad because our cardiovascular training decisions are mostly based on the phrase "FIVE DOLLARS DOWN TO START!" Let us think of ourselves as a bold, brave, exciting new club—pioneers into the diversity of the twenty-first century!

What is a Bargain Health Club? If you find yourself waving a cosmopolitan and saying to a group of linen-clad people, "I just joined the L.A. Sports Pavilion—it's terrific," yours is not a Bargain Health Club. A true Bargain Health Club (which will tend to have names more like Bally Total Fitness—aka the Health Club of the People) is not for Conspicuous Exercisers, say those of the culturally imperialist Westside, where flat-bellied investment bankers jog smugly down the boulevards with Evian bottles and sleek, Iams-fed red setters trotting at their sides.

I'm not saying I don't wish I could *afford* an A-list health club. I'm not saying I, *too*, wouldn't enjoy a facility where I could enter a shower stall without fear of embarking on some kind of hideous Voyage to the Planet of the Hairballs. (Or as a Korean lady grunted at me yesterday: "Don't go in there. Ants.")

But I prefer it this way, I really do. I feel great about my nineteen-dollar-a-month health club (or my "health violation" club, as my ~~older sister Kaitlin~~ busybody officemate Maribeth so unkindly put it), in its seedy North Hollywood minimall. Because every time I go, I get to rub elbows with the real L.A., the future of America, the fastest-growing demographic groups in this country. . . .

Who are—? Think about it. The eighties fitness boom is *long* over. Never mind if many of L.A.'s surviving fitness facilities—with their Vegas-y neon signs, digital rowing machines, gleaming Nautilus gear—still call to mind the young, the fit, the Spandexed, the *Perfect* (in the narrow John Travolta/Jamie Lee Curtis sense). By now these folks have retired their headbands, gained twenty pounds, had three kids, moved to Valencia.

No. *These* days, who actually still has the five dollars, the interest, and the three hours in the middle of the day to attend daily step classes? At my Bargain Health Club, two great tribes:

1. The Eccentric Elderly
2. The Wildly Foreign

Or they may combine—e.g., the tiny wizened Latino man I saw the other day leaping about in homemade, space alien-ish "protective goggles" fashioned from wraparound sunglasses, tinfoil, string. Above him a flashing pink neon sign enthused, "Racquetball!"

You see? The Bargain Health Club stands for no less than cultural liberation, creative individuality, justice. Ten years later, is it not, finally, the RTD Bus/Lucky Plastic Bag crowd's turn to have their way with discos that used to be our *Sports Connections*? Is it not the people's turn to ride the StairMaster? Oppressive rules, regulation athletic wear, deodorant foot spray, swimming in just one lane . . . why?

Speaking of which, let's talk about our seniors. Note that in overpriced, Stalinist Westside athletic clubs (circular front drives, valet parking) there *are* no old people. In that scary "Baby Boomer Fearing Fifty," *Logan's Run*–type way, "old" behaviors are forbidden. You may be a sixty-four-year-old man, but you act forty-five—doing a fast treadmill, reading *The Wall Street Journal*, secretly making sure there is no nose hair. Verbal references to the aging process are tasteful, Bill Moyers–esque. (Wrong: "My back is going." Right: "I've always wanted to explore **Tai Chi**.")

At the Bargain Health Club, seniors can totally let their hair down (or their oddly shaped toupees, as the case may be). What results is a veritable celebration of curmudgeonly behaviors, like:

1. Suddenly yelling out at the aerobics instructor: "Feh! My knees!"

2. Men: Carefully putting down paper towels on the locker room floor and walking on them. (That's how they avoided athlete's foot during the Depression, they will tell you.)

3. Women: Using Lifecycles not so much as cardiovascular trainers but as kitchen stools to sit on, not pedaling at all, while watching *Oprah* with a friend (in saggy 1957 bathing suits) and complaining.

4. In the swimming pool: Wearing plastic floral swim caps and wandering into the lanes of others while loudly complaining. Hanging onto the metal step-railing and kicking wordlessly, with a dour expression, for hours at a time.

Notice, further, how some people in L.A. talk a great talk when it comes to cultural diversity—but have secret limits? They will donate money to refugees in China, yes, insist on fresh coffee from Kenya, profess delight in the miserable Bolivians who clutch tiny pockmarked instruments on our outdoor Promenades.

But . . . will they shower with them? I think not. With our narrow Western thinking, we still think of ideal women's locker rooms as clean, gorgeously tiled places through which Summer's Eve–type women in snowy white towels laconically drift.

I am proud to shower with The Other, to revel in the cultural safari that is my "steam room." Let me describe it.

Under a sign that commands *NO LOOFA SPONGING* sits a

trio of sixty-five-year-old Asian women in sweat-soaked gray underpants loofa-sponging as though it is their last day on earth. (Idea for a PBS series: "Asian Culture: Love Affair with the Loofa.") Other (expressly unpermitted) steam room "liberties" taken include grunting, slapping, the sudden release of the saggy bathing suit top, causing the huge veiny breasts to fall out with a *plop*, the vigorous shaving of wobbly calves, the aggressive filing of horny toenails (while wincing, as though in pain).

Whew! It is all enough Celebration of the Primal Self some-times to make me want to run home and eat an entire box of Entenmann's. Which just means the next day, of course, I have to go . . . right back to the gym.

<attachment #3>
3. I don't know about YOU, Anita, but the following was a New Year's resolution <<I>> made this year. While I know Amelia.com's stated mission is to stress the positive and self-validating aspects of the Internet, at its heart, I think this is a piece about the quirks and foibles of modern life Amelia.com subscribers all live with, and will certainly be able to relate to. Laughing at ourselves is sometimes the best medicine, is it not? (Perhaps for the FunnyZone? Unfortunately, could not open that particular webpage—it kept crashing and flashing "ERROR MESSAGE 103, INVALID DECODER.")

Say "No" to Funny E-Mail

I admit this is but a *small* step for mankind, a *small* way to clean up my own very *small* corner of the planet, a *small* line one *small* person draws in her own *small* box of sand, but here it is, my New Year's resolution: No more "funny e-mail" (and that's in quotes) will be accepted at this address.

That's right. Go ahead. *Add* me to that list of fifty and mass-*forward* me that list of unfunny lawyer jokes or how many Bill Gateses does it take to screw in a lightbulb jokes or Top Ten Signs You're Marv Albert jokes or whatever else you pulled off the Internet . . . sitting there at work as you are, coffee souring in its mug, in the middle of your boring day at boring silicon.techno.edu.despair.com.

You thought you'd scoop up a shovelful of "funny" and fling some at fifty of us, did you? Well, get this: I'm not going to take it lying down. I, better known as Sandra46@aol.com, am not just going to click "Delete" and move on. No, I am actually going to take the time to type you a personal note informing you that I actively reject you. Personally.

(Further, if you're hungry to incite dramatic political action . . . do try to do more than hit a single computer button, while seated at home in your sweatpants. I'm thinking, recently, of the panic my Blocked Writer friend Jolene flew into because of a new bill she heard about on campaign finance reform in Massachusetts, blah blah blah, Republican Congress, blah blah blah, "And I was stunned to see, on MSNBC, this former federal prosecutor who told this panel show host that—"

I didn't get through all of it—it was a three-thousand-word missive that had to be downloaded in three chunks and kept crashing in the middle and, still, all of us on her e-mail list are supposed to add our names to the bottom. . . .

And I'm thinking, This is kind of a lazy person's protest, isn't it? *Before*, we had the Boston Tea Party, which involved getting out of the house, the bumpy carriage ride to the harbor, the donning of costumes. *Now* what the hotheads among us are saying is: "I saw this thing on cable the other night and I was so irate I typed an e-mail! And then I . . . *forwarded it!*" I mean, is a simple *march* too much to ask for anymore? I don't know.)

Anyway, back to the problem of the Amazingly Unfunny.

Before you mass-forward that next list of jokes . . .

First let me ask you the abstruse philosophical question: What is the nature of "funny"? "Funny" is in the eye of the beholder, that's true. And yet for centuries we've had ways in society—and that is the point, *in society*, among *people*—of telling whether or not *we* are funny. How can we tell? We ask ourselves the following questions: "At parties, do my friends' eyes light up when I enter the room? Do they lean forward in excitement when I launch into what I think is a funny story? After I finish, do they laugh, clap me on the back, and say these words: 'Oh my God, Stan, you are so funny'?"

If the answer is no, you are probably *not* a funny person. People do not enjoy your jokes. Now, I realize that telling a joke to a roomful of ten people is not exactly the same as mass-forwarding a list of twenty jokes to fifty people you went to college with fourteen years ago, people you consider your "friends" . . .

Which brings us to another question. What is a "friend"? Some people think of "friends" as "people to interact with in some meaningful way." Others—*you*—apparently think of "friends" as "a passive data base of computer addresses for mass-mailing unfunny jokes, uninteresting newsletters, and unattractive photos of my unattractive baby in his unattractive hat."

Speaking of which, and here I refer to the deadly family Christmas newsletter ~~my obscenely boring and didactic ex-college roommate Carl and wife Sumiko~~ you mass e-mailed us, the face-less fifty, lo this past December, what possible use can I have for the information that your two-year-old daughter, Kimmy, learned to say "cat" in March and that your four-year-old son, Timmy, learned to tie his own shoes in April? I have never met or seen these children, except via computer screen, in the blurry website photo you attached, and thank you for that, because you moved to Seattle—and you never invite me *there* to visit, you never come to *L.A.* to visit, because of the conviction that contact with this fetid city would somehow pollute the perfect biosphere that is the tiny family you are holding hostage—home-schooling will be next, I'm sure—in your architect-designed compound in the isolated woods of Washington—

I mean, maybe I'd be interested in Kimmy and Timmy if you ever once asked me *anything* about my own life these last ten years, I mean *anything.* You might discover that besides learning to say "cat" in 1965 and tying my own shoes, with great style and verve, for thirtysomething years already, I've done many *other* things, too. But no, you just want to mass e-mail stuff *out:* You do not want to get anything back *in.* The Unabomber: It is you. And you know what? I don't care what GUIs you added. *I wouldn't visit your family website if it was the last place on earth.*

In short, my friend, when you mass-forward us that next list of unfunny Internet jokes, realize what we, the fifty faceless members of the data base, will hear you very well indeed. Oh, you—you're the guy at the end of *The Fly* wobbling in a sticky web and saying: "Help me! I have nothing to say!"

Or maybe you just thought the jokes were funny. Um—either way.

Contents:
1 Internet Message Header
2 <no topic> *Binary*
==================== Begin Part 1 ====================
Topic: Internet Message Header
Format: LATIN-1

Sender: abanning@amelia.com
Received: from chewbacca (therep.dsl.speakeasy.net [216.231.46.110])
      for <Sandra46@aol.com>; Fri, 17 Mar 10:47:10 -0800
Reply-To: <abanning@amelia.com>
From: <abanning@amelia.com>
To: <Sandra46@aol.com>
Subject: New Column for Amelia
Date: Fri, 17 Mar 10:50:48 -0800
Message-ID: <0101bf3b63$d1118290$be1514ac@chewbacca.
      womezone.org>
Content-Type: multipart/mixed;
      boundary="----=_NextPart_000_0011_01BF3B20.C2EE4290"
X-Mailer: Microsoft Outlook 8.5, Build 4.71.2173.0
X-MimeOLE: Produced By Microsoft MimeOLE V4.72.3110.3

Dear Sandra,

Thanks so much for your submission. For your perusal, here are some notes from our recent editorial meeting regarding the three pieces you sent us.

The Zone Diet
Funny! We can use as is. And God knows we all feel that way.

Bargain Health Clubs
We can use this, with a few changes. In particular, a few editors felt uncomfortable with the "loofah sponge" section—approximately 20 percent of our target subscribers are Asian-American, and part of our mandate includes not presenting minorities in any manner that could be construed as negative. (Also, one of our advertisers *is* Bally's, so, of course, that reference will need to be altered.) (We also have some free

coupons in case you would like to change your health club—apparently the Bally's in Encino is a little less grody.)

<u>Say No to Funny E-Mail</u>

Funny, but several editors felt the tone was too "edgy," "harsh," or "extreme" for Amelia.com. In fact, one of our editors burst into tears when she read it. (Apparently she has two children who happen to be exactly two and four, and the two children happen to have their own website; it's complicated.)

But I understand your interest in writing something about the wild woolly Internet. My suggestion is that you look at the Funny-Zone piece (type in "ab:45%*&" when it crashes—should get you in) dated January 12 by Carol Ann Marbles on wacky animal websites. Carol Ann Marbles (you might remember her hilarious if short-lived column "La La Lines" in the Health section/Hughes Market/back page/automotive insert of the *L.A. Times* "Southern California LIVING" section) tends to have more the tone we're looking for in terms of women's humor.

What I propose is that we start you on a weekly first-person column (we thought a fun name would be "Foibles"), on a six-month trial basis. The pay will be one thousand dollars a week. I'll FedEx you an advance for the first two columns on Monday. Within the next month, we will be asking you to come down to the BFG Los Angeles studios to read these columns on camera—at the very least, we will immediately begin using this content as part of our twenty-four-hour live webcast "streaming."

Also, we've just begun development talks with Fox on a range of possible new Amelia.com television projects—Denise Francis will keep you updated as we go.

That's it for the moment. And of course . . .

WELCOME ABOARD!!!

—A.

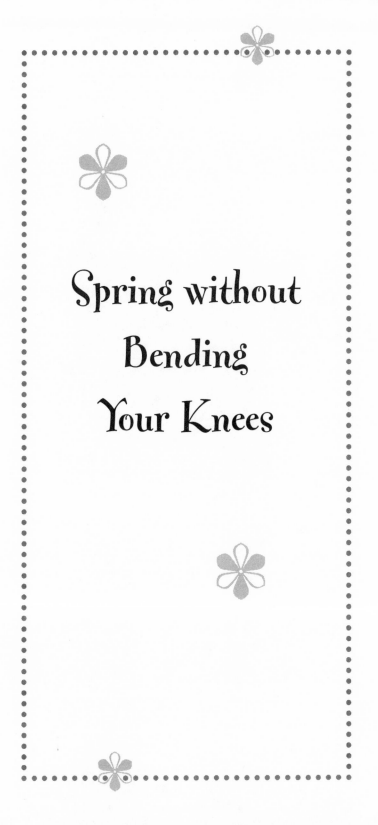

Spring without Bending Your Knees

March 21

11:02 a.m.

Temperature: 76 degrees

West Hollywood, Brian's House, Rose Garden

●

Third morning of a several-month stint house-sitting and dog-sitting

at the gorgeous home of my corporate lawyer friend Brian, who,

with his screenwriter boyfriend Paulo,

has gone to Tuscany on a fabulous walking tour, which features

wine-tasting, cheese-sampling, and gazing at frescoes

(to, in Brian's words, "experience the quality of the light").

I turned down his offer of five hundred dollars a week

because I'm rich now and life is fabulous.

●

The Secret Lives of
Married Women

"I n Tuscany," Brian has written to me, on an elegant art deco postcard, in his trademark flowing hand, "it is *lavender-gathering* season. Paulo and I sit together on the piazza this morning sipping fresh-brewed espresso. Before us, across rolling, mist-tipped hills, the air is heavy and almost drunken with the slightly spicy scent of crushed branches and herbs. . . ." I skim quickly on. "Curl of woodsmoke . . . Fragrant panettone . . . Mellifluous low of distant cow . . ."

"Well, Brian," I'm tempted to write back to him, as I review the next letter in the stack, "according to your comptroller, Kenneth P. Berger, 'In Los Angeles, it is *tax* season. . . .' "

Such a variety of mail Brian gets! No wonder he needs me to sort it every day. There are missives from the West Hollywood city council, missives from APLA, multiple Sundance Store catalogs, multiple Territory North catalogs, and—

Hello! What's this?

The new April issue of *Playgirl* magazine.

Playgirl magazine? Oh Brian, you didn't! I think to myself, chuckling.

Playgirl magazine, I think to myself later, as I water Brian's antique rosebushes. I mean, if *anyone* should be turned on by such fetid, shameful material, it would be me. After all, here I am, a red-blooded woman in my mid-thirties—supposedly my sexual peak—in the first of five months apart from her husband. That's right—due to a fellow sax player's sudden illness, Ben snagged a last-minute gig playing "Jazz Favorites" (a category loose enough to include not just the rich compositional oeuvre of Kenny G but such diverse voices as Kim Carnes and Andrew Lloyd Webber) on a Calypso Line "Jazz Cruise." Total artistic debasement, yes . . .

But for a shiny fifteen hundred dollars a week! Ben and I actually clinked champagne glasses to celebrate—then went serious. "It'll be hard," I said. "Really hard," he agreed, squeezing my hand.

Of course, I couldn't help noticing that when I dropped my beloved off at his drummer friend Jim's, he literally *ran* toward the van—suitcases, garment bags, fanny packs of "funny tapes for the road" flying. His fellow band members seemed giddy as lottery winners (which, I guess, at fifteen hundred dollars a week, they are). As the van pulled away, there was vigorous high-fiving, blowing of the horn, the sudden loud crunch ("Oops!") of a car stereo. . . .

How refreshing it is to flee the site of a Depression! I couldn't help thinking. Even for me—and, for the last year, I've been the *vessel* of that Depression. . . .

Because, wow, what an explosion of energy *I* had as soon as Ben left! And, my God, what a lot there is to do around Brian's sunny, European countryside–like house! For the past three days, I've been watering plants, opening shutters, closing drains, letting pool people *in*, letting gardeners *out*, feeding Lord Casey (Brian's fifteen-year-old pug) his carefully calibrated Iams meals and his incredibly complicated array of pills!

And best of all, after racing around West Hollywood to drop off and pick up splendid racks of stunningly expensive Hugo Boss dry cleaning (drop off! pick up! drop off! pick up!), I've been getting takeout dinners, every single night, from Koo Koo Roo! Which since it's in West Hollywood, on Santa Monica Boulevard, is like the *gay* Koo Koo Roo! (The Gay Koo Koo Roo! Sounds like the witty milliner hero of some high-stepping Restoration comedy!) Which is perfect for me, because newly single as I am, the only "chicken" I'm going to get is roast *Koo Koo Roo* chicken, which, guess what, is ON THE ZONE!

Even an *entire roast chicken*, which I've taken to eating, in traditional Single Person style, right over the sink! "Can't talk long, honey—I promised the guys I'd watch this new BBC comedy show with them on the ship's satellite!" Ben yells at me his first night away, over a crackling long-distance line. "Knock yourself out!" I yell back, waving a Santa Fe–style chicken leg, scepterlike, over a veritable mini-kingdom of Koo Koo Roo side dishes flung grandly out along the counter—macaroni and cheese, creamed spinach, de-cobbed corn, mocha-fudge brownies. Envious? Not me. I'm on a little cruise of my *own!*

That's Ben and me: Married People on Vacation . . . from our Marriage! What kind of vacation? *Separate* vacations! The very best kind!

Don't get me wrong. Ben and I love each other dearly. Being Married to each other is as wonderful as Marriage could ever be—

But the hours! No one—no parent, no chaplain, no priest—ever warns young impressionable people about the sheer *hourage* during a week Husbands and Wives can expect to log together. I mean, when I used to live with my own *sister*—as overstimulating a person as you could ever hope to meet—we used to *hit* each other just to pass the time.

Of course, Ben and I don't hit each other. No. What we do is *support* each other, support, support, support, support. . . .

I mean, Ben wouldn't have forbidden me from eating any of those things—those Koo Koo Roo things. No, it would have been:

"*Eat* that macaroni and cheese, sweetie. Why not? You deserve it. As a matter of fact, *I'm* going to have some, too. Okay! We're eating macaroni and cheese now. And feeling good about ourselves. *I* feel okay. Do *you* feel okay? I think we *both* feel okay. Okay!"

Because that's what Husbands and Wives do. They talk about food. What else is there to talk about, after almost a decade? You've covered all the *big* stuff: life, death, love, money, family, commitment, hopes, dreams—you basically agree, it's been signed off on. . . .

Actually, I've noticed that in recent months, Ben and I have spent a lot of mornings (after he's finished his "real" papers) discussing the *L.A. Times* "Valley" section. How bad it is, how full of peculiar items that pass for human-interest stories—or, as Ben calls them, "human noninterest stories." For instance (cover story, top half, above the fold), recently there was a big oak in Encino, apparently . . . *that was cut down.* That's the whole story. *It was cut down.* Said a baleful woman to the *Times* (huge color photo, caption): "That tree was my best friend!"

"There's such a thing as too little stress," Ben observed.

The other drastically underpublicized activity central to Married Life, I find, seems to involve lying on the phone for the other person. I myself bring a natural enthusiasm for the medium. In my temp days (of the Ross for Less jacket), everyone said I was a fantastic secretary with a great phone voice—I'd always answer the phone and sing out: "Marvin Carroll and Associates!" In conversation, I'd make everything sound like a *narrative in motion,* as though every thought was preceded by the phrase "Interestingly enough . . ." They'd go: "Can I speak to Marvin Carroll?" I'd go: "Marvin's not in today, but . . . ?" Or I'd say: "I don't think the FedEx has *come* yet, but I'll be sure to check. . . ." Sometimes I'd go a little wry with it: "No, we *don't* need new office furniture, but thanks so much. Your name is . . . ?"

Plus, I'm quick on my feet. One afternoon, we got a phone message from Callie, an unstable New Age chick singer, reminding Ben about a fifty-dollar bar gig starting at ten o'clock that night in Orange County. My job was to call back immediately and say that, sadly, Ben was going to have to cancel at the last moment because he was just coming in from New York and his plane was . . . (waving barbecue tongs, in a floppy boxer-short swimsuit, Ben mouthed the words at me) "GROUNDED IN A SNOWSTORM IN DENVER."

Then the chick singer calls *back,* saying she doesn't *know* any other tenor sax players in L.A. she can call at the last minute and is seriously freaking out (sound of screaming on the phone, jagged sobs). Well, I get that plane right back *up* (via a terrific new shuttle service called Mountain Express—a fortuitous new partnership allying Southwest Airlines, United Airlines, and a little-known hourly transfer service of my own sudden invention called Boulder High Air). Impressed with the heroic effort, Callie beeps back considerably more mellow, admitting she probably doesn't *need* a fourth horn in an eleven-piece band . . . And suddenly that commuter plane is *down* again in Phoenix. (Wing problems.)

By contrast, over the years, whenever I try to get Ben to lie on the phone for me, I am reminded, once again, tragically, that I have *not* in fact married the gay male assistant of my dreams. Ben seems to get stage fright: Put a phone in front of him and he's like the proverbial deer frozen before the Peterbilt.

"Um, Sandra . . . ? She's lying around in bed right now," he'll mumble as I wave my arms wildly, tapping a pad upon which I've written helpful phrases like "Buried under a twenty-four-hour deadline," "Snowed in in Tuolomne Meadows," "Horrible food poisoning—errant ling cod on Ventura Blvd." "She won't come to the phone," he'll say dourly. "She's kind of out of it."

Truly, the texture, substance, and feel of Marriage is really *so* different than advertised. I have illustrated this in the following charts. . . .

"FIREPLACE MOMENTS": aka: WARM LITTLE MOMENTS OF OUR LIVES (GLASS OF WINE IN EVENING, FOOT RUBS, WITTY DISCUSSION OF DAY)

CHEERFULLY CREATING A CUTE HOME TOGETHER: COOKING GOURMET MEALS, PICKING OUT LAMPS, FLECKING EACH OTHER PLAYFULLY WITH PAINT

SPIRITUAL STUFF (COUPLES' YOGA, ETC.)

OUTDOOR ADVENTURES (KAYAKING, HIKING IN ROCKIES, HOT-AIR BALLOONING)

MAKING TIME TO EXPLORE EVER NEW CREATIVE WAYS OF SEXUAL EXPRESSION (AKA: KEEPIN' IT FRESH!)

IDEAL TIME SPENT TOGETHER BY A MARRIED COUPLE

"FIREPLACE MOMENTS": aka: WARM LITTLE MOMENTS OF OUR LIVES (GLASS OF WINE IN EVENING, FOOT RUBS, WITTY DISCUSSION OF DAY)

CHEERFULLY CREATING A CUTE HOME TOGETHER: COOKING GOURMET MEALS, PICKING OUT LAMPS, FLECKING EACH OTHER PLAYFULLY WITH PAINT

OUTDOOR ADVENTURES (KAYAKING, HIKING IN ROCKIES, HOT-AIR BALLOONING)

SPIRITUAL STUFF (COUPLES' YOGA, ETC.)

MAKING TIME TO EXPLORE EVER NEW CREATIVE WAYS OF SEXUAL EXPRESSION (AKA: <u>KEEPIN</u> IT <u>FRESH!</u>)

<u>**ACTUAL** TIME SPENT TOGETHER BY GAY MALE COUPLES</u>

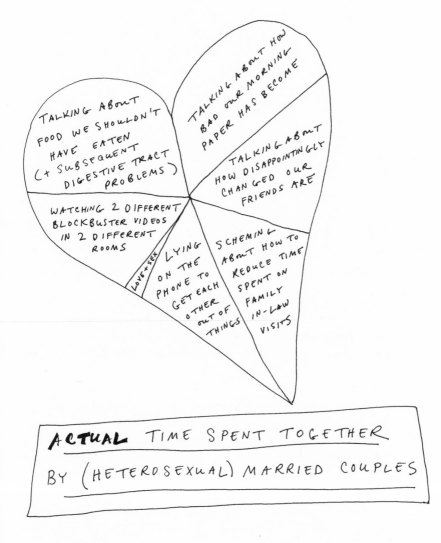

ACTUAL TIME SPENT TOGETHER BY (HETEROSEXUAL) MARRIED COUPLES

I'm not kidding about the gay couples! Look at Brian and Paulo. Unlike Ben and me, they have actual vibrant interests, hobbies, things they do together. Wine-tasting in Napa, flying to Paris to take a Cordon Bleu cooking course, hot-air ballooning over the Loire, jetting to India to explore a new kind of yoga where one has to hold the ankles of the other, and press lovingly on the points, or the chakras, or whatever. . . .

Of course (and here I feel just the faintest stab of resentment as I pour myself a lead glass tumbler of Arizona Iced Tea, bottles upon bottles of which live in Brian's knotty pine–paneled Sub-Zero refrigerator), why _shouldn't_ Brian and Paulo be living a life of bliss?

They've got air miles. Tons and tons of air miles!

I mean, sure, Ben and I could _try_ to fly to India to find our points and our chakras, but it would be on the worst international flight in the world. We're talking a Costa-Gavras/human-rights violation of a flight. The leg from L.A. to New York alone would take thirteen hours. Why? Because when you're poor and disorganized like us, your "travel agent" is Cheap Tickets. No matter how close the destination—San Francisco, heck, _San Diego_—Ben and I are always flying out of LAX at five A.M. (The Super Shuttle people are always saying: "Okay. LAX. Reno Air. We'll be there to pick you up at, whoa, two-fifty A.M.!")

And _why_ do we have no air miles? Because Ben and I have the worst VISA card in the world. Rhode Island Credit and Loan. The photo on the front is of a horse pulling a cart in front of a tiny red barn. Very picturesque but . . . is this the kind of slow-moving iconography you want for your VISA card? (What imagery did the art directors _discard?_ A dial telephone? A Morse code machine? A wooden outhouse with a crescent moon?)

You look at this dented piece of plastic and think: This is a VISA card that does _not_ command Respect. Or Rewards. I mean, all around us, 24-7, triumphal people are winging around with Platinum cards (they even have their own magazine—_Platinum!_— I saw it in Brian's guest bathroom), they're getting first-class air miles, spending money and making even _more_ money the faster they spend it. . . .

As all the literature suggests, clearly, a really great VISA card is supposed to help you:

Soar like an eagle!

Buy a lot of tennis balls and hit them against the wall, laughing!

Have lobster in Sydney with a man not your husband!

One's VISA card is supposed to be like a silver sword, a magic chalice! It's supposed to inspire Respect . . . but more important (my eyes narrow sagely) Fear. Waiters give you bad service when you're using the magic VISA card, and not only are they punished, they are BEHEADED. On television. Before thousands. They are SHAMED!

Indeed, sometimes I think I don't care if I never have sex again, as long as I get to fly first class for the rest of my life! Unlimited miles, no restrictions, SAS, Air France, never Tower . . . *and* a limo, back and forth to LAX.

No, that's extreme. Let's say instead of the Platinum plan, downgrade to the Gold plan. You know, fabulous sex four times a year with someone you care about, pleasure yourself the rest of the time as needed—business class, unlimited miles. And maybe not a limo but a Town Car. And then, for those of us lower-brow folk who live in the Valley, perhaps the Bronze plan. Fabulous sex four times a year with someone you love, throw in another six to ten sort of average episodes where one person's not really in the mood—you know, those times where one spouse says to the other, "Go ahead without me, sweetie, I'm not really sure where my mind is this month"—Town Car, *and* business class, maybe only out of Burbank—

Oh, fuck it! It all . . . just makes me want . . . to look at Brian's *Playgirl*!

I've done my chores, I'm reading *Playgirl*!

I know it's loathsome, but that's what I want to look at right now: *Playgirl*.

I plump myself down on a wicker chaise longue, push all the catalogs aside, flap the damned thing open.

Okay. Okay. I'm looking at it.

I'm looking at the centerfold—former Madonna dancer and

model Angel Ortiz. So okay. He looks exactly like what you'd think a former Madonna dancer named Angel Ortiz would look like. Long greasy hair, gold earrings, shiny pecs . . .

Mr. Ortiz is photographed in an array of the usual positions. There are tousled sheets, there is oil, there is the scantiest of G-strings (one that, if I may say, takes the "G" out of string), a difficult-to-parse narrative involving chain mail, a fair amount of sultry gazing, and the occasional grabbing of the male ~~Mamber~~ Member.

For the record, Angel Ortiz is an *attractive* man, fit and also surprisingly *limber*, no question there. But beyond that . . . when looking at these Naked Dance Poses—Angel is here, Angel is there, Angel is wet, Angel is hungry, Angel is upset—I find, as a woman, that I am feeling less titillation than nervousness. I mean, if you've had *any* experience out there in the dating field, you know that the sight of an oiled, eerily hairless man with an earring posing tempestuously on a bed is generally not promising.

If you're anything like me, you might even sigh to yourself: "Well, it's gonna be a long night." A long, enervating night.

Because after the minimum of pleasuring—if any—is done, a lengthy bedside discussion is sure to follow *about* one Angel Ortiz, his latest headshots, should he switch managers, what can you do for *him?* (Maybe even an angry tirade will follow: "Zat Madonna—vy dazzn't she cohl me any mo'? Because aff my pooled 'amstreeng? Eet eez bettair now, zo match bettair!")

And here is the more fundamental, more nagging question: "What kind of man would want to pose, naked and oiled, for a glossy magazine?" The mini-bio strains to argue that this is a man who *really loves women* ("My fantasy is doing it on a beach, with champagne, with a lady with hips, real hips"). But I don't think so. The only men I know who would enjoy posing in the nude are bodybuilders, struggling actor/models, or . . . well, guys who are gorgeous and gay. And there's nothing wrong with that. It's just—I hate to go out on a limb here, but I can't believe a gorgeous twenty-five-year-old *gay* guy would truly enjoy having sex with me (thirty-five years old, 152 pounds, female).

And what about my own husband? I think suddenly, in alarm.

Here he is, off for five months—*five months*—on a cruise. (A "cruise"—it's literally called a "cruise" . . . !)

I'd tried to call Ben last night, via the incredibly complicated set of international codes he gave me, but all I got was this dead, flat buzzing sound. I hadn't thought twice about it, assumed it was only a matter of time before he'd ring me . . . but he didn't.

He only called me the first night. And now it's night number three.

Which gets me wondering. When that honking van pulled away from the curb the other day, what exactly was it Ben felt he was leaving behind? After all, what has his wife—what have *I*—become over the last few years? A blocked, bedridden writer. Some joyless stay-at-home. A harridan in sweatpants. A mandala of soiled coffee cups, crumpled tissues, despair . . .

By contrast, who's to say *who* one meets on ocean cruises? My God, who and what?

March 27

8:49 p.m.

Temperature: 75 degrees

West Hollywood,
Brian's House, Kitchen

●

Oscar Telecast

●

Oscar Telecast

'm standing in my sweatpants and slippers in Brian's kitchen. I'm vigorously mixing chunks of Iams dry dog food with moist, gluey Pedigree Beef and Liver and generous swatches of Koo Koo Roo chicken skin—it's this kind of ultra high-protein paste I've devised for Lord Casey's dinners. I mix and mix and mix—it's harder work than you think, to get the chunks smoothed out. You have to really concentrate. On the small portable TV on the counter, the Oscars are on, a wash of diamonds and tulle and celebrity emoting—there's a weeping Gwyneth Paltrow, a shell-shocked Ralph Fiennes, looking slightly stunned in his tux . . .

"And in the feature-length documentary division, the Oscar goes to . . . *My Kosovo!* Monica Veerklausen, director."

In ABC Super Slo-Mo, I look up from my green Tupperware of chunky dog paste. But no, I've heard the announcer correctly. There she is, Monica "Little Brown Wren" Veerklausen . . . the familiar braid of frizzy brown hair, the sackcloth tent dress, the Birkenstocks. And yet impossibly beautiful this evening, touched by divinity, cheeks shot through with pink, glowing, radiant, weeping.

"Icy Stab," I scream. "Icy Stab!"

I stagger heavily, like a Mafia don fatally shot, toward the cordless. With trembling fingers and rapidly waning life force, I tap out the well-worn number. But Ruth isn't in—Ruth's service says she is at a Silent Retreat in Big Sur, unreachable for weeks.

76

"But I'm having an Icy Stab!" I protest. "This is an emergency!"

"Uh, okay . . ." the woman at the service says. There's a rustle of papers. "You must be Sandra?"

"Yes!"

She dutifully replies: "The note here says you're supposed to remember that you are a . . . toad in a labyrinth and that it's all just cave paintings. Does that help?"

Making these sorts of lowing, bellowing sounds—"Ahh! Ahh!"—the cry a calf makes when fatally hacked in the belly—I hang up and tap out the digits for Ben's cruise ship . . . satellite number . . . through the international operator . . . who's somewhere in Belize. It's like 011 . . . 37 . . . 952 . . . our AT&T calling-card number . . . xxx . . . pi to the eleventh power. . . .

But I know it's hopeless. I'll never get through. My husband is having an affair with a six-foot-tall Brazilian stewardess and it's hopeless.

My back to the wall, I phone the very last number. . . .

"Okay," I say, my voice wobbling with effort. "You say you want me to always phone you right away with my crises. But I'm telling you, the reason I don't is that you're a terrible listener."

"I listen!" Kaitlin cries out, indignant.

"You listen . . . but you never *hear*. You're totally judgmental. You never say the right thing back. You always manage to come up with remarks that are the exact *opposite* of comforting. Whenever I call you, I hang up even more stressed than I started."

"You do?" She seems honestly surprised—as if this possibility has never occurred to her.

"So let me tell you the story," I say, "and then I'll tell you exactly . . . how . . . to respond. All right? Then I won't hang up upset."

"Okay!" she agrees, trying to mollify me. "Okay."

I take a deep breath. I go in.

"So . . . Monica Veerklausen is this ex-classmate of mine from the Graduate Writing Program at USC. . . ."

"Graduate Writing Program at USC," Kaitlin repeats carefully. "I hear you. I am hearing you. See how I'm hearing you?"

"Okay," I cut her off. "Let me go on. The point is, Monica Veerklausen was always this Little Brown Wren of a person, deadly serious, we used to *laugh* about it, how serious she was. . . . I mean, she was always trekking off to Somalia on her own dime to do, like, volunteer work for the hungry and shoot eight-millimeter video of the death camps for the Peace Corps or something . . . and *then* I guess she must have hied herself off to Kosovo and filmed some kind of one-hundred-thirty-seven-minute documentary because tonight, eight years later, there Monica Veerklausen is, standing at the Dorothy Chandler Pavilion before a billion people . . . *winning a fucking Oscar!*"

I sink my head into my hands, hyperventilating.

"So . . . good for her, right?" Kaitlin's voice comes through the receiver, uncertainly.

"Don't speak," I say.

"O—" Kaitlin stops herself mid-syllable.

I return unbound to my own special Technicolor, 35-millimeter World of Misery. "I mean, I know I'm this total failure at age thirty-six—"

"Oh, come on!" Kaitlin bursts out. "You're not thirty-six."

"In one week I *will* be!"

"What are you doing for your birthday?" she answers back. "With Ben out of town?"

"Ohhh . . ." I say evasively. "Big party, you know. Jolene and Ted and the others. Mexican restaurant in Silverlake. Salsa dancing. Karaoke singing with a drag queen named Raoul. Whatever." I slump back down again. "Anyway—I know I'm a failure and I'm okay with that . . . the knowledge that I'm old enough now that people I went to college with are accomplishing huge things. You know, I read in my alumni newsletter how so-and-so wrote a very well-received book on macroeconomics. No problem. Or somebody else is vice-president of Arco. Fine. Who cares?"

"Who cares," agrees Kaitlin.

"But with little Monica Veerklausen . . ." I continue. "I didn't even know she was in the running! And suddenly she has an Oscar! For doing her Art! And Tom Cruise—and all of Hollywood—is applauding her! Meanwhile, the high point of *my* year has been getting hired by a women's website that keeps crashing to write a little tiny column about my stupid little life called 'Foibles.' " I pause. "I'm going to slit my wrists."

"May I speak?" Kaitlin asks.

"Y-y-yes," I say. "But notice, in review, that the theme is *not* 'Monica Veerklausen—good for her!' We *do* wish her well in the abstract, yes, but this is not *about* the triumphs of Monica Veerklausen, it's about the woe of me. You know, the tragedy of a life wasted/blah blah blah/etc., etc. Okay: go."

"I know exactly what you're saying," Kaitlin says. "And I agree."

"You do?"

"Yes!" she exclaims. "Sure! Every time I watch the Oscars, I *too* think, Why am I not up there? Why am *I* not winning an Oscar?" Her voice turns from wonder into outrage. "On my deathbed, I think *I'd* kind of like to have had that experience! Why should I somehow be denied that? When exactly was the turning point in my life when I said no to . . . the whole Oscar thing? Maybe not for acting, but maybe for directing—like you say—a documentary!"

I remind you that Kaitlin is a high-powered financial consultant who makes a zillion dollars a year. She went straight from Stanford into a huge MBA program into the six-figure-a-year job that she has had ever since. She has never known one moment of sacrifice, or hardship. I remind you of the Marin townhouse. The ever-splitting stock. The perfect size four. Kaitlin's idea of hardship is driving a year-old Saab (which, by the way, she never has to do due to her corporate never-drive-a-year-old-Saab [fucking "Platinum"!] lease program).

"When did you say no to winning an Oscar?" I erupt. "Try *over the last forty years!* When you've never *once* bothered to pick up a camera! Not even one of those Polaroid One-Step thingees! Not even at my own *wedding!* You don't even know how to load film!"

"In filmmaking, the director has someone *else* load the film," Kaitlin declares, unperturbed. "They're called gaffers, cinematographers, boom boys."

"Oh, where did you read that?" I cry out. "In *Meg Ryan Fan-wagon Magazine*?"

"What?"

"Never mind."

"The point is," Kaitlin says, "you don't need to know how to load film to make a movie. To have some kind of . . . Academy Award—worthy . . . filmic vision."

"Oh, please! You know damned well someone like Monica Veerklausen knows *how to load her own film!* Indeed, I seem to recall that Monica Veerklausen can give vaccinations, do CPR, drive a six-axle bus! I remember this . . . this endless slide show Monica gave at the Town and Gown at this fund-raising dinner we all had to go to! One that I tragically . . . nodded off in the middle of." The memory of it hits me—suddenly, clearly. I see my whole destiny crystallizing at that moment. I *nodded off.*

"Because Monica Veerklausen," I realize aloud, woeful, the full weight of it finally hitting me, "she's just . . . *Oscar material.* Pure and simple. Some of us are, some of us aren't. With all that time she spent in Kosovo, she probably even knows what Katyuska rockets are," I mumble, flashing back on the CNN debacle as if it were a Vietnam. "And those . . . B-12 bomber thingees."

"Well, frankly, I don't think the odds are all that impossible," Kaitlin persists. "I was reading in San Francisco *Focus* how in the documentary categories, there are less submissions. So maybe they only *have* ten or fifteen or twenty submissions for the Oscar in the first place. And making a documentary—how hard could it be? The subject matter is right there in front of you. Buy a camera, get some . . . gaffer-type person to load it—"

"Kaitlin!" I am screaming into the phone. "Don't you see? YOU COULD NEVER WIN AN OSCAR! YOU COULD NEVER WIN AN OSCAR! You have to live in a mud hut without electricity! In Kosovo! For eight years! And shoot heartbreaking video every day! And eat grub! And not ever, for a moment, expect to *win* the Oscar! Because in that moment, you will totally . . . lose your focus. Indeed, the moment you specifically set out to *win* the Oscar, well, that's the moment your entire project is doomed!" It's like my Congo novel! I find myself realizing. As soon as

I won that award, got that fax, saw that glittering avenue of fame and promise stretching out in front of me, I couldn't write another word!

But I can't tell my sister that. She's even more shallow than me!

"Don't you see, Kaitlin?" I yell in frustration. "Monica Veerklausen, us. Monica Veerklausen, us. Two totally different tribes of people!"

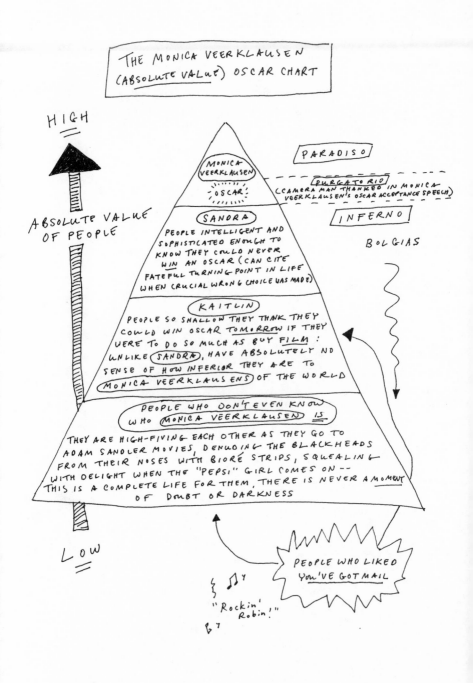

THE MONICA VEERKLAUSEN (ABSOLUTE VALUE) OSCAR CHART

HIGH

ABSOLUTE VALUE OF PEOPLE

PARADISO

MONICA VEERKLAUSEN

OSCAR

PURGATORIO
(CAMERA MAN THANKED IN MONICA VEERKLAUSEN'S OSCAR ACCEPTANCE SPEECH)

INFERNO

BOLGIAS

SANDRA
PEOPLE INTELLIGENT AND SOPHISTICATED ENOUGH TO KNOW THEY COULD NEVER WIN AN OSCAR (CAN CITE FATEFUL TURNING POINT IN LIFE WHEN CRUCIAL WRONG CHOICE WAS MADE)

KAITLIN
PEOPLE SO SHALLOW THEY THINK THEY COULD WIN OSCAR TOMORROW IF THEY WERE TO DO SO MUCH AS BUY FILM: UNLIKE SANDRA, HAVE ABSOLUTELY NO SENSE OF HOW INFERIOR THEY ARE TO MONICA VEERKLAUSENS OF THE WORLD

PEOPLE WHO DON'T EVEN KNOW WHO MONICA VEERKLAUSEN IS
THEY ARE HIGH-FIVING EACH OTHER AS THEY GO TO ADAM SANDLER MOVIES, DENUDING THE BLACKHEADS FROM THEIR NOSES WITH BIORÉ STRIPS, SQUEALING WITH DELIGHT WHEN THE "PEPSI" GIRL COMES ON -- THIS IS A COMPLETE LIFE FOR THEM, THERE IS NEVER A MOMENT OF DOUBT OR DARKNESS

LOW

"Rockin' Robin!"

PEOPLE WHO LIKED YOU'VE GOT MAIL

April 2

Temperature: 75 degrees

West Hollywood,
Brian's House

●

My Thirty-sixth Birthday

●

Now We Are Thirty-six

10:11 A.M.

Ben is on the line from Belize.

"Happy birthday, sweetie!" he calls out cheerfully. "Did you get the big package I sent?"

"No," I say. "Did you send a package?"

"Shit." He puts his hand over the receiver. There is angry discussion. All I can make out are fragments like: "FedEx?" "DHL?" "International zip code?" "Packing number 100439-27?"

"The codes are horrible here," he swears. His voice becomes worried. "Plus, I think I gave you a wrong digit for the long-distance number. If you want to dial the ship, I think you have to press in a four *before* the three rather than after. And then maybe also a star *before* the one. Everyone here has been having trouble with . . ."

And all at once, my faithful husband is back. I feel a great weight lift off me.

"Never mind," I tell him. "Your mom sent a package. A medical bracelet that lists my allergies in case they find me unconscious somewhere, a box of bracing caffeinated teas, and this sort of black flannel sleep mask."

"A sleep mask?"

"Actually, I'm kind of excited. I've always wanted to try a sleep mask. Your mom and I talked about insomnia for . . . oh, about a hundred and seven minutes."

"I'm so sorry," Ben groans. "She is *such* a monologist."

"Oh, I don't mind," I say—and I don't. "In his den, Brian has this amazing three-deck Solitaire game on his computer . . . *and* a convenient clip-on telephone headset. So really, I could have listened to Dolores for another four hours. It was very relaxing—watching the cards fly across the green background, stacking up the aces, changing the backs of the deck from a tropical-fish pattern to a sunburst pattern to a—"

"Well," Ben prompts, a bit gaily, "I hope you're going to do something much more Fun than that for your birthday!"

There's a beat.

"Fun," I muse, philosophical. "What is the nature of Fun? For some—for instance, for those of us who are twenty-three—a night of Fun requires a college kegger with a skate-boarding dog and karaoke singing and a limbo contest run by Jagermeister gals in bikinis. For others—say *me*—a night of Fun involves three Emma Thompson videos, the Santa Fe Chicken plate from Koo Koo Roo, all the Tylenol PMs I want, a pitcher of vodka and Diet tonic, in bed by eleven. Coup de grâce? Your mother's sleep mask. I can't tell you how excited I am to try out this sleep mask."

"No," Ben says.

"Yes," I say.

"You have to have a party or something!"

"A party?" I say acidly. "Do you remember a certain *New Year's* party that I—"

"Have you called Ruth recently?" he cuts in.

"Look," I declare wearily. "Ruth is away, I forgot the disks for my novel in Van Nuys (which is fine because, as we all know, I probably wouldn't be working on it *anyway*), Monica Veerklausen just won an Oscar. . . . Do you understand, Ben? For the moment, at least, Game Over. And so, as a *birthday treat* for myself, for one month, I'm abandoning all efforts at Personal Growth. I'm giving up on all of my Personal Growth Projects. One of those types of Projects being, as we know, the throwing of too-ambitious parties, and their resultant Shamu-like flopping."

"You have to do *something* for your birthday," he insists. "I know how much birthdays mean to you. You have to get out of the house or you'll have a mood plunge. You have to see people. You have to celebrate!"

"Frankly . . . I don't see what there *is* to celebrate. I mean, turning thirty-five was bad enough. Turning thirty-five was cataclysmic!" The morning I turned thirty-five, I hurled myself facedown on my bed, clawed the pillows, gave forth Medea-like howling. Because from then on, I knew I would be forever *marked* as thirty-five—all puritan and sexless, with all those awful medical/Lifetime Channel–ish/baseline mammogram implications.

And then, of course, I famously insisted that we go to this Zagat-praised restaurant (Shallots on Melrose) for dinner, but the day had already been so fraught with tension/Medea-like howling/clawing of pillows/etc. that now *Ben* came down with *sympathetic* stomach cramps, but this restaurant was *so* exclusive, they said they were going to charge us a cancellation fee even if we *didn't* go, so all of a sudden we're spending two hundred dollars on an absolutely horrible evening where Ben has to excuse himself every ten minutes to go vomit and I'm thinking to myself, I'm thirty-five years old and still being dissed by snotty maître d's at mean restaurants where the valet parking is fourteen dollars! Is it because . . . all we have is this lousy Bank of Rhode Island credit card? That's it! It's this goddamned credit card!

In a snap, the elusive promise of the sleep mask has evaporated and suddenly I'm back smack dab in the middle of my Technicolor World of Futility.

"How great are birthdays, anyway?" I ask Ben, my voice going shrill. I feel one of what he calls my "yammering attacks" coming on, but I'm sorry, today I'm powerless to stop it. "Really, the last truly *happy* birthday an adult ever has is twenty-one! Twenty-two and twenty-three go by in a blur, and then you hit twenty-four! Twenty-four is mixed. You know why? Because twenty-three is the last year a person can officially be considered a wunderkind. Twenty-three is the last year you can be photographed for *Details* magazine in black leggings/at an art gallery/electric guitar/Sean Lennon/funny glasses . . ."

"What?" he says, distracted.

"You know what I mean," I say. "There's this certain kind of cool photo of a young creative person suddenly flaring up out of nowhere that simply *will* not work after the age of twenty-three. Then you turn twenty-five, 'quarter of a century,' you joke, and yet deeper angst is starting to gnaw. The Olympics, for instance. In . . . like . . . sprinting. *That* door is forever closed to you, at twenty-five! Or Wimbledon. People winning that are like sixteen, seventeen. How did this happen? These wraithlike moppets in ponytails, whipping by! Then come twenty-six, twenty-seven, twenty-eight, twenty-nine, and then . . . thirty. And then it's *really* downhill. . . ."

4:51 P.M.

Spirits rallied. I've gone to the corner (hip, gay) video store and rented:

1. *Remains of the Day* (takes place in picturesque England)
2. *Sense and Sensibility* (takes place in picturesque England)
3. *Enchanted April* (takes place in picturesque Italy—with added bonus of the comfortingly be-gloved and be-hatted Joan Plowright)

I've got a pharmacy's worth of Tylenol PMs (but also, I've noticed in Brian's medicine cabinet, Xanax) (I've not yet gotten into the Xanax but am thinking about it), I've got a huge icy vase of Absolut Kurant vodka, a big bottle of Oceanspray cranberry, and even some cherry-flavored Nyquil. (Being a chronic insomniac, I'd be lying if I said I'd never considered trying an icy nightcap made of Absolut vodka and cherry Nyquil, but I've nixed the idea as too *Valley of the Dolls* for someone who is neither Shelley Winters nor whose current profession is *not* "hoofer on Broadway.")

In any case, add a coupla pints of Ben and Jerry's, a war chest's worth of things Koo Koo Roo, a new flannel sleep mask, and . . . who needs a trip away? It's my *own* little *Year in Provence*, right here on the kitchen counter.

The doorbell rings. It's just before five. Maybe it's finally the FedEx, I'm thinking. Maybe it's Ben's package.

I go downstairs, open the hatch to look out . . . and start screaming.

"No!" I yell. "Not you again! No! No! No! No! No!"

"Open up!" Kaitlin yells back. Like some kind of horror movie Birthday Clown, she is sporting a spray of balloons and a flame-red, sharp-coned party hat.

"How did you even find this house?" I moan. "How did you even know the address?"

"Ben called me. He gave me the coordinates. He was worried."

"Goddamned Ben!" I mutter. I continue to yell through the hatch: "Listen, Kaitlin. I didn't invite you to fly down here. And I'm not letting you in. The last thing I want, on my thirty-sixth birthday—to remind me I'm one foot in the grave—is a goddamned birthday party—"

"This is not a birthday *party*, this is a birthday *intervention*," Kaitlin threatens. "Think of me as a birthday SWAT team. I have horns. I have cake. I have streamers. I have tear gas. You have no choice."

Canny weasel that she is, Kaitlin has also brought a Birthday Hostage. She thrusts this Hostage forward. Her voice goes eerily chipper.

"And to add to the festivities, I've brought along Gwyneth from Accounting. Remember Gwyneth, from the company picnic? She was nice enough to fly down from San Francisco with me. She was generous enough to drop her Wednesday-night plans to come party with us. Isn't that nice? Say hello to Gwyneth."

Oh my God, I think, Gwyneth. When I'd been first introduced, my automatic reaction was to start to say: "Oh—you mean like Paltrow, the actress!" but the words died on my lips. Because, Gwyneth from Accounting? She's like . . . *Gwyneth Paltrow's molecular opposite.*

I close the hatch and open the door, beaten at my own game.

"Hello, Gwyneth," I say dutifully. "How are you? How have you been? How's the—the sciatica problem?"

Gwyneth from Accounting steps in. She is a savagely morose

woman with gray troll-doll hair. She's built like the cartoon character Broomhilda. Her saggy eyes perpetually look like they're
about to brim over with tears. As mentioned, the sciatica. Discor-
dantly, she wears tight yellow slacks and a San Francisco Giants
windbreaker.

"I know how you feel about birthdays," Gwyneth says in a
monotone. "Just had one last week. Turned fifty-three. Where
have the years gone? I need a drink." Fifty-three? She doesn't
look a day under seventy-four. Gwyneth's fireplug body moves
forward into the house. Her baffled, slightly dazed expression
does not change. The small white hamhock arms lift up, reaching
forward, like a douser, as though feeling their way toward
the drink.

Kaitlin sweeps in after, businesslike, a swirl of balloons and
hats and streamers and cake. "I'm sorry," she hisses, as a distant
clatter signals that Gwyneth is out of earshot. "I really wanted to
bring my friend Harry, who is *so* much more fun, but Harry had
some sort of rhythmic drumming class tonight and Gwyneth was
standing *right there* in the hallway, overhearing our whole phone
conversation, and then she suddenly offered to fly down with me,
and I couldn't say no. Gwyneth has had this *really* tough month.
Her Chevette was totaled and her cat died."

8:17 P.M.

The three of us stand together in Brian's Italian farmhouse–
style—if luxuriously appointed—kitchen. Huddled under a forest
of dangling copper pans, we've gone through most of the grocery
cake, all of a large Domino's pizza, and are well into our fourth
pitcher of screwdrivers. In Gwyneth's case, she has poured a little
of her screwdriver *over* her cake and mixed it together to make
kind of a screwdriver slushy, an inch-wide strip of which is
smeared on her chin. Things are gettin' drunk and ugly.

Kaitlin and I, as we often do, are screaming at each other
about the all-consuming matter of My Sad Money.

"The point is, you're thirty-six now—almost forty!" Kaitlin's
haranguing me. "Which means you need to start being more

proactive about your money! Have you even set up a retirement account? What financial plans do you have for retirement?"

"Retirement? Retire from what?" I yell back at her. "Last time I checked, my career hadn't even *started!*"

"All the more reason to plan for your future."

"My God, Kaitlin! Not all of us can be *you*—a person who's been thinking about retirement ever since she was twelve!"

"I have *not* been thinking about retirement ever since I was twelve!"

"Are you kidding? You were the only kid on the block who used a beach bucket as a piggy bank."

"Well, *you* were the only kid who used her piggy bank as a fishbowl."

I am stung at the unfairness of her accusation. "I was nine, for crying out loud! The thing with the fishbowl—it was totally by accident, and just the one time!"

"Was not!"

"Was so!"

"Was not!"

"Stocks!" My bullying big sister grabs me by the shoulders, her hand a vise grip. "You need to get into stocks! Do you know your cousin Stanley just became a millionaire? His company, Micro Tech, just went public!"

"Of course he's a millionaire!" I shout back. "Every time I open the paper, I read about some twenty-two-year-old kid who's a millionaire . . . *on paper!* That is, they'll be millionaires *when* they become fully vested in four years, and *if* their high-tech stock stays as high as it was *last* week at a dizzying sixty-four dollars a share, AND! IF! BUT! WHY! HOW! WHEN! WHERE! WHO! Of course, the company could fold, the stock could plummet, one could lose twenty thousand dollars in a day. . . . At which point, if you're like me, you'd be forced to hurl yourself headfirst onto the bed, tearing your hair out, and shrieking, Medea-like: 'I'm dead! The end has come! I'm a horrible, tragic failure!' "

"You'll go *broke* if you don't put it into stocks!"

"How can *that* be?"

"By the time you retire at sixty-five—"

"Again with the retirement!"

"—inflation will have accelerated faster than interest rates. You see? For people your age, low-interest investments are the riskiest kind. You see, dummy?" She punches me in the arm. "When will you get it through your thick skull? You'll actually *lose* money if you don't invest it in high-risk stocks with high margins and high yields—"

"The little money I have is not retirement money!" I snap, pulling myself loose, punching her back. "It is not investment money. It is not high-risk money. This is money of the Now. This is money of the Moment." Earlier in the day, I was playing Brian's soundtrack from *Rent,* so I feel I can almost hear a kind of pulsing rock score behind me. I raise my arm in a *Saturday Night Fever* salute. "This is money that *feels* and *does* and *is* what it wants to be . . . NOW. It is simple money that just wants to sit down sometimes and smell the flowers or take a Monday off and read a book! This is money that sometimes likes to go pantless because it feels really breezy! Come on, K.! You leave my laconic, under-achieving, poorly performing, crappy-interest money alone!"

"Oh my God!" Gwyneth cries out, snapping our attention to her. She closes her saggy brontosaurus eyes, clenches her pudgy fists, yields up a five-screwdriver cri de coeur:

"Do you ever have the feeling your husband is the *last person on earth* you want to have sex with?"

Kaitlin and I stare at her, in horror.

Gwyneth barrels messily on, with her Unwanted Information:

"I mean, sometimes I go through a day and every man I see— *literally every man*—the loan officer at the bank, the FedEx guy in the truck, the eighteen-year-old Vietnamese kid who pumps gas at the 76 . . . I feel like I'd have sex with any man I see— *anyone* . . . before I'd ever do it again with my husband!"

"Euh," Kaitlin and I say, in unison.

"You know how long Sengupta and I have been married?" Gwyneth implores. Sengupta? "Twenty-three years. Twenty-three years! Good Lord! It's not like our sex life isn't amazing—I mean, he wants it all the *time*, every position, all over the apartment. We just came back from this Advanced Tantric Sex Retreat in Ojai where—"

"Okay, Gwyneth, okay!" Kaitlin says, raising perfectly manicured fingers in her patented "Tell it to the hand" motion. I close my eyes. I, too, am trying to block out the image of Gwyneth running wild through the streets of San Francisco, nude, lusty, possibly oiled, trying to mount everything in sight like a small, plump schnauzer.

But the force of Gwyneth and her unbridled sexuality is unstoppable.

"My God, after a particularly active weekend, sometimes my crotch is so sore I need a *sitz bath*—"

"All right, Gwyneth, all right," Kaitlin says. "We get the point."

"But the monotony!" Gwyneth cries out. "The sheer monotony . . . of always the same man! Sometimes I feel like I should have been born into another culture, man." The drunker she gets, the more this latent Santa Cruz hippie cadence in her speech starts to come out. "Even in America—where, let's face it, everything is so restrictive—I think even in America, husbands and wives should be handed three 'Get Out of Jail Free' cards. You know? Coupons you can redeem for exactly three affairs. Three free affairs—no muss, no fuss, no consequences."

"Well, that would have helped out greatly in my *last* marriage," Kaitlin murmurs drily, sloshing another twelve ounces of screwdriver into her lead glass tumbler.

"I mean, *marriage*, man," Gwyneth groans. "The sheer monotony of it. The sheer monotony. Sometimes I feel that monogamy is like this . . . five-thousand-pound anvil I want to put down . . . just put down for a moment!" She closes her eyes. She plants her sturdy tennis shoes apart, bends her legs, chubby in their sweatpants. Balls up her fists. "I just . . . want . . . to put . . . the anvil . . . of monogamy . . . down!"

We stand together, for a moment, in a malodorous silence.

I come to first.

"Geez, Louise," I mumble uncertainly. "Look at the time—"

"And last night," Gwyneth blurts out. "Last night I had this incredibly hot dream about Ralph Fiennes!"

"Oh, God . . ." Kaitlin places a hand over her size-four stomach.

"But here's the weird thing," Gwyneth butts on. "It wasn't Ralph Fiennes of *The English Patient*. I'm talking Ralph Fiennes, thirty pounds heavier, as the sullen Nazi in *Schindler's List*! He has me in the basement. I'm all tied up—"

"That's it," Kaitlin announces. "We're going back to the hotel." In one swift motion, she grabs our sweaty-faced satyr by one of her flailing hamhock arms.

"I'll walk with you," I surprise myself by saying. I reach out to pin Gwyneth's other flailing hamhock arm, as we force her into her oversized San Francisco Giants windbreaker.

Kaitlin, Gwyneth, and I walk together, swaying slightly, through the quiet, residential streets of West Hollywood. The traffic from Sunset sounds muffled tonight. The sky is purplish. The scent of gardenias lays heavy on the streets. The air is cool on our cheeks.

"Harvey Keitel—doesn't he live in Los Angeles?" Gwyneth is babbling. "I'd love to do him! He was so hot in *The Piano*! Doesn't he live in this neighborhood? I bet we could knock right on his door."

"Tylenol PMs," I tell Kaitlin. "In my pocket. About six of them should put her right down. So she doesn't go banging the door down to Harvey Keitel's. Or Regis Philbin's. Or Dom DeLuise's."

"Speaking of sexy dreams," Kaitlin remarks. "Last week I had this sexy dream . . . and my ex-husband *was actually one of the guys in it.*"

"Your ex-husband?" I say. "Now, *that's* really weird."

We open the gate of the small, exclusive West Hollywood residential hotel they're staying in. Its leafy front walkway twists like a . . . a maze. A maze of hedges. A garden labyrinth. The darkness of it is odiferous, pleasant. A distant windchime tinkles from some private greenhouse. Well, I'm thinking, if Ruth's labyrinth were anything like this, walking it wouldn't be such a chore. It

would be more like . . . falling, falling, falling . . . into the center
. . . of some hidden . . .

9:43 P.M.

I've deposited Kaitlin and Gwyneth in their rooms. I'm looking
forward to collapsing in my own plushy bedroom, back at
Brian's—among Martha Stewart linens, a snoring Lord Casey, the
sleep mask. Five hours of drinking and I am practically stupid
with exhaustion.

But pushing open the lobby door, I once again smell those
gardenias, hear the tinkle of that windchime . . .

Some subtle omen? Apparently yes. Because it seems my day
is still not done.

A hand grips my arm.

"Sandra?"

I turn.

"David . . . Long?" I erupt in surprise. "What are you doing here?"

"The magazine," David Long says, wavering. His tie is askew.
His pale thin hair is tousled. Even in the dim, refracted yellowish
light of the lobby, he looks utterly smashed—like I am. "Everyone's here: the whole gang. We had a party for Shirley." He indi-
cates the glassed-in bar beyond, a fishbowl of familiar faces,
talking, laughing, clinking wineglasses. Shirley is the New York
publisher of a movie magazine I used to work for. David was—and
apparently still is—the senior editor.

"You remember *Shirley*, of course," David adds, in more of
a . . . a throaty purr.

"Is she still the star of her own movie?" I find myself shoot-
ing back, equally sly.

David leans in, conspiratorial, shoulder pressed to mine.
"Unfortunately, it's a *Henry Jaglom* movie."

"Oh David, you're terrible!" I squeal, mock-slapping his arm.
In turn, he grips at my hand and . . .

If I *did* have an affair, I suddenly think, if I did have access to
one of those itchy little "Get Out of Jail Free" cards, I don't

believe I'd *choose* one of those high-maintenance Angel Ortiz
Madonna dancer types. No, I'd take a discreet, understated, wryly
witty type like . . . the man gripping my hand.

I mean, let's face it. The short time I'd edited at that magazine, I'd always had just a teeny, weeny little bit of a crush on
David Long. He's one of those sandy-haired fortyish guys who's
tall, slim, and sort of . . . Connecticut-looking. (Aka: the polar
opposite of Ben, who, while adorable in his own way, has flyaway
dark hair and a thickening middle.) David Long looks just a
teeny, weeny little bit like Kevin Costner. In a tweedy jacket. With
leather elbow pads.

Okay, a little more tense. A little more worried. Picture David
as this *slightly* tense, worried-looking Kevin Costner who's also
losing a little of his hair—

But he's *hilarious* about it—that's the saving grace. About the
balding, he used to demur, "Living up to my college promise,
when my hairline was voted 'Most Likely to Recede.' " All those
funny little jokes we used to have, elbow to elbow in the mail-
room, all those wicked little—

But of course, not only is David Long married, he seems essen-
tially too shy, too reserved, too bottled-up-in-his-feelings, too—

And suddenly, right there, David Long leans forward and
gives me a quick hot kiss on the mouth.

"Oh my God!" I hear myself mumbling drunkenly. "I'm
stunned."

"Oh yeah?" he says, with a kind of odd aggression, as though
gearing up for a fight. "Why are you stunned?"

"Well, because I'm . . . not the sort of woman men make
passes at. . . ." Especially not on a night like this, I think, suddenly realizing what I must look like—no makeup, hair in a ponytail, clad in . . . in sweatpants. And here David works for a *movie
magazine*, for crying out loud. He has continual access to *Baywatch* babes and VH1 babes and Victoria's Secret models, yon
eerie beauties who hover coolly, like ice particles in the ghostly,
shiny rings of Saturn, beyond the vast, rocky asteroid belt of the
rest of us—that is, we ever-present, always available, always on
time, enthusiastic if perhaps a tad chatterboxy batik-skirt women

who spill out over bookstores and Democratic fund-raisers and UCLA Extension creative writing classes everywhere.

Ben keeps assuring me there *are* no *Baywatch* babes on his Jazz Cruise. . . . He says he has yet to see a female in a swimsuit who's under one hundred. (And now the long-distance code works perfectly fine, and we've already talked three times today, and . . .)

At the same time, one can't be too sure. I mean, what if Ben—

"Are you thinking what I'm thinking?" David asks huskily, his face inches from mine. With one hand, he strokes a tendril of hair from my temple.

"What are *you* thinking?" I ask, distracted by the Victoria's Secret women.

"I'm thinking we should go . . ."

I wait, honestly curious to see what he's going to come up with.

"I think we should go to my car," he finishes.

"To your *car*?"

"Uh-huh," he says, leaning heavily, even a bit tiredly, into me.

"You want us to *have sex in your Camry*?" I ask, appalled.

"No, no, no," David says, growing slightly irritable. "Nothing like that. I just want to, you know, neck a little. For an hour. That's all. You'll be home by eleven."

And that's how I spent my thirty-sixth birthday! I can imagine proudly telling my grandchildren years later.

"C'mon," he repeats, tugging at my arm, like a small boy. "Let's go. I can put the seat down."

"Oh my *God*," I say, trying to convey *moral* outrage, but in truth what is hitting me like a slap is the sudden sense memory of David's car. David drives a blue Camry station wagon that always smells slightly of fries. If memory serves, was there a—was there a child's *car seat* in the back? A *Sesame Street* car seat? With cartoon characters?

"Come on," he says, tugging again at my arm, sullen.

"Oh, *please*, David," I say, pulling completely away from him, and he reaches back and I grab *his* arm in response and this time my grasp is not at all flirtatious but most definitely that of a nurse on her patient—firm, strong, even *warning.* . . .

Suddenly we're having this strange kind of . . . *tussle* in the walkway. At the same moment, I feel his strength waning. After all, he's drunk, he's exhausted, he's running out of steam. Too soon, I know, this fragile bubble of ours will burst under its own weight anyway. A gale of laughter echoes, distantly, from the magazine party (especially one high laugh—one familiar-sounding, sharp, cawing, slightly irritating woman's laugh . . .).

The fact remains that, before I release him utterly, I want to know just . . . one little thing.

Which is: Why, of all the glamorously dressed and made-up women here tonight, did David Long come out of the lobby and pick me?

Why didn't he lunge drunkenly instead at, say, Lisa, the little copy-editing intern from UCLA? Lisa from UCLA! We used to laugh about her, round the office. Very well-meaning, very blond, very young (twenty-three). She was fixated on David—on his wry, opaque, quasi-intellectual Kevin Costner—ness, I guess. She'd listen to him talk about Alain Resnais films with these . . . big wide eyes. (And that laugh! That irritating laugh! My God! Caw caw caw caw caw!) Lisa's crush on David was cute and we all used to joke about it, but at some point, all this David and Lisa, David and Lisa stuff had sparked this bolus of irritation—

Which I realize now, like a headache, is gone.

Because, hideously awkward as his pass has been, the revelation here tonight is that all these years *David has clearly been thinking about me.* Simple as that. Elemental as the weather. Birds . . . and bees . . . and fish . . . gotta swim. Etc., etc. Poor man. He just couldn't help himself.

"Oh, come on," I purr, conciliatory. I open my arms and be-drape David Long with a generous helping of Second Prize—the gift of forgiveness, maternal warmth. Daring to go even further, I slip an arm through his, like an eel, and give his hand two pats—pat, pat. I steer him gently toward the street.

"I know things have been tough in your marriage and your

home life for a while," I murmur. Now it's my lips that brush his ear, intimate. "Let's walk around the block. Get some air. Talk this thing through. You and me."

"Okay," David Long mumbles, nodding, obedient. "Okay."

We begin a grand tour around the block, David and I, the Mature Woman He Longs For But Can Never Have. Lit-up faux-Tudor-style homes and lawns and cacti gardens float dreamily around us. Within the warm cocoon of Us, I gently pull out the skeins of troubled thoughts that are inside of David. . . .

He's been depressed about turning forty, he says, they're taking a second mortgage on the house, he should have a novel of his own published by now. . . .

Yes, I'm thinking, but that's always true. That's perennially true. Who doesn't have an unpublished book project like a stone around their neck? Blah blah blah blah blah. The question remains: Why did he cross the line with me today? Why is tonight different from all other nights?

And in a thunderbolt I realize: It's this new L'Oreal eye cream I've been experimenting with from Brian's medicine cabinet. It's supposed to radically reduce the appearance of under-eye bags. Looking in the mirror every morning, I'd come to the conclusion it wasn't having any effect, but thank God I kept using it. . . .

Because clearly it did something. It worked. In about three weeks. (Which is about how long these beauty things are supposed to take.)

How do I know it worked? Because today . . . David Long . . . saw someone new.

And suddenly I feel my whole world opening. For so long, I realize, I've been shuttling along this grim, dingy tunnel toward forty, air stale, walls narrowing, possibilities closing. But now, with a beauty product that is actually the miracle it said it is, a beauty product that actually turns back time . . . !

"Uh-huh, David," I say huskily, as he babbles on. "Of course, all of us serious writers find it frustrating, what with the shift in the fiction market, and opportunities for mid-list novelists shrinking. . . ." I'd like to see "Lisa from UCLA" try to follow this conversation, to keep up with the adults!

"Michael Chabon," David pushes on, his voice taking on the traditional keening, whining sound David Long's voice sometimes takes on, when he's had too much to drink. It's the pitch I'd sort of forgotten about, and I feel this stab of annoyance, but there's no stopping David once he gets going on his favorite subject. "Michael Chabon," David rails on. "His first novel gets published at twenty-four! Twenty-four!" (This happened over a decade ago and the insult is as fresh to David as if it were yesterday.)

And I'm thinking, How did this happen? The first time in *years* a man makes a pass and he's as depressed and self-involved as me. My God! He's my evil twin!

"And what's Chabon's book called?" By this point in the monologue, David is absolutely unstoppable. *"The Mysteries of Pittsburgh! The Mysteries! Of Pittsburgh!* That's a weighty novel idea for you!"

How our flirtation is like this little clown car! Unless the two of us are pedaling frantically *in the same direction at the same time,* it doesn't go anywhere. . . .

"David!" I say, demanding, finally, that he focus on me. On *me.* I've slogged far enough through this exhausting conversation, and this soggy walk, and this soggy arm-holding, that I deserve one thing. My frickin' . . . *compliment.*

"David," I say. I clear my throat, soften my voice. Try to approximate my earlier purr. "Just tell me this," I say. *"You're* married. *I'm* married. If it's just necking in the Camry you wanted, why didn't you ask Lisa?" I try for a sultry Natassja Kinski pout—or, at least, do the best I can. "I mean, I'm a fellow *writer,* after all. I'm complicated, I'm difficult. . . . Why in the world would you risk everything to . . . ?"

I lean in. I wait. I tilt my L'Oreal-smoothed eyes back to maximize the flattering effects of the evening light.

And David leans his head back and wails, gutturally, at the moon:

"Because Lisa didn't . . . come . . . to the party!"

Contents:
1 Internet Message Header
2 <no topic> * Binary *
==================== Begin Part 1 ====================
Topic: Internet Message Header
Format: LATIN-1

Sender: abanning@amelia.com
Received: from chewbacca (therep.dsl.speakeasy.net [216.231.46.110])
        for <Sandra46@aol.com>; Thu, 4 May 10:47:10 -0800
Reply-To: <abanning@amelia.com>
From: <abanning@amelia.com>
To: <Sandra46@aol.com>
Subject: "Foibles"
Date: Thu, 4 May 10:50:48 -0800
MIME-Version: 1.0
Content-Type: multipart/mixed;
        boundary="----=_NextPart_000_0011_01BF3B20.C2EE4290"
X-Priority: 3 (Normal)
X-MSMail-Priority: Normal
X-Mailer: Microsoft Outlook 8.5, Build 4.71.2173.0
Importance: Normal
X-MimeOLE: Produced By Microsoft MimeOLE V4.72.3110.3

Dear Sandra,

Good job on the in-studio videotaping, and thanks for your recent batch of submissions.

I laughed out loud while reading your hilarious piece on canker sores, and also the one about the vomiting pug. While I'm not sure we can use these, thanks for sending. The rest, in some edited form, will work fine.

As we're preparing our big Summer Preview Beauty and Fashion Launch (we're aggressively pursuing a new slew of advertisers, including some biggies like *Vogue* and Lancôme), the editorial committee has asked if you could do a couple of pieces on Summer Beauty and Fashion? Perhaps your funny take on sunscreen, or on the "new" DKNY bikini (have you seen this thing? it's really quite wacky!). As long as it falls under the rubric Summer Beauty and Fashion, anything will be fine.

Best,

A.

—————

Sender: Sandra46@aol.com
Received: from imo24.mx.aol.com (imo24.mx.aol.com [152.163.225.68])
    by spdmgaac.compuserve.com (8.9.3/8.9.3/SUN-1.7) with
    ESMTP id PAA04465 for <abanning@amelia.com>;
    Mon, 8 May 15:14:27 -0500 (EST)
Message-ID: <0.8ed03f7c.2572e71d@aol.com>
Date: Mon, 8 May 15:14:21 EST
Subject: May columns
To: abanning@amelia.com
MIME-Version: 1.0
Content-Type: text/plain; charset="us-ascii"
X-Mailer: AOL 4.0 for Mac - Post-GM sub 54

Dear Anita,

Thanks very much for your note.

I understand Amelia.com's impulse to focus their editorial more on Fashion and Beauty. Although I do not consider myself an expert on Fashion and Beauty, I'm enclosing an excerpt from my own journal, which we might be able to cut down into a couple of 750-word pieces.

I find myself, as a woman who just turned thirty-six, increasingly obsessed with aging. And I'm sure your subscribers are, too. Here is an I think humorous take on the subject I think everyone will be able to relate to.

Best,

Sandra

The Eye Bag Chronicles
● ●

1. The Invisible-to-Society
(aka Little Brown Wren) Eye Bag

g don't know exactly what it is—*and I'm not sure I want any-*
one to tell me—but over the past few years, I've started to
notice that I . . . no longer get approached by strange men.
For directions, for the time, for a lift, for a cigarette, for . . .
(cue a husky deepening of the voice) . . . for anything.

I'm not saying I truly crave the attention of the Strange Men
in the world: yon thick-bearded fella in line in the single-serve
deli section, yon slump-shouldered twentysomething CompUSA
sales youth, a neighbor, a postman, a businessman, a moving man,
bag boys, busboys, pool boys, winos, no—

All I found myself thinking the other day, in a sudden stab of
injured vanity, was:

Why has this ozone layer of male pestering suddenly been
removed? Is it because I've drifted into that dark female conti-
nent called . . . (once again, cue husky vocal deepening) . . . over
thirty-five?

I'm not saying that in my giddy "salad days" I was anything
like a Stone Fox. No. But at least when you're twenty-three, with
your ponytail, and your jeans, comically balancing groceries on
your little red hatchback, cans of tuna rolling every which way . . .
somehow people's faces just . . . *light up* when they see you.

My friend Jolene remembers that when *she* was twenty-three,
hurtling up and down the streets to her oh-so-important-at-the-
time newspaper job in her coat and her scarf and her boots,
construction workers would always wave and yell things like:

"Smile, honey! It can't be *that* bad!"

Men . . . don't say that anymore.

"I run around with the exact same expression on my face,"
she says. "But now, 'cause I'm forty-one, they assume it *is*
that bad."

My own seventy-nine-year-old dad takes another tack. Every time he sees me, the first anguished words that fly out of his mouth are:

"Oh, Sandra! You look tired! You are under a lot of stress, eh?"

This has been my dad's traditional greeting for, oh, the past *nine* years. Weddings, anniversaries, book readings, theater premieres, floods, fires, whatever—it's all a blur to him. The only image etched startlingly clear in his mind, over and over again, is of me hunched over like a crow, a picture of exhaustion.

Recently I've started coming back with:

"Actually no, Dad, I'm feeling particularly well-rested and terrific! It's just, *this is what I look like,* at age thirty-six. What I think you *mean* to say is: 'My God, Sandra! You're looking so old and *haggard!*' Let's practice that word together, Dad, shall we? *Haggard.*"

2. The Empowered Eye Bag

A week later, I go to dinner with my ex-boyfriend Bruce.

Understand that for as long as I've known him, Bruce has been a vegetarian, nonalcoholic, Buddhist-meditating, colon-irrigating . . . Basically, he's unemployed.

(Also, a parenthetical, re: the colon thing? I ask you: Is it logical to imagine a God who would create a human body in which eyes, ears, synapses, red blood cells, corpus callosum, islet of Langerhans—everything works beautifully except for one thing: You have to put a tube up your butt once a month and flush out your colon?)

Anyway, so true story . . . Bruce is telling me he has recently become so weak and dizzy, he finds he can barely sit up straight on his yoga pillow. Because he does not traffic with regular doctors in the Corrupt Western Medical Establishment, to see what's wrong, he sends some strands of his hair to this Oriental medicine commune in Illinois where they check it for mineral content and pH content and whatnot and even *they* say: "Are you a man? You need to eat some meat! My God."

And I remember, as Bruce was saying how now he was trying to get his $225 back from the commune . . . I remember I did something new. I tilted my head back, relaxed my face, and fixed him with this expressionless, mid-focus gaze. It was a gaze that plainly said:

"Maybe I'll raise my eyebrows in surprise and concern, maybe I won't. Maybe I'll squint my eyes in Active Listening, maybe I won't. Because you know what, Bruce? Maybe your problems aren't worth *wrinkling my face over* anymore. You think about that."

3. The Competitive Eye Bag

Now it's Thursday, and I'm having lunch with some of my old female magazine cronies. We used to get together to gossip about people we knew and jobs we had, but now, of course, careening toward forty on balding tires, all we talk about is our aging faces.

"It's not the *aging* that bothers me," says my friend Diane. "I'm not that shallow. You know, crow's-feet . . . I'll take crow's-feet any day! Crow's-feet signify lots of smiling, joy! Add the Barbara Bush pearls, the big silver mane, and people will say:

" 'What laughter and loving you've enjoyed in your many rich years on this planet! Just seeing your weathered beauty is an inspiration!' But no, with me it's: 'Are you stressed? Are you tired? You look terrible.' "

And so recently, Diane informs us, she has begun collagen treatments. In the . . . chin. That's right. Diane is obsessed with her chin. She thinks she has a sunken old chin.

"My doctor is fantastic," Diane says. "Dr. Howard Gleiberman. Harvard-trained. He's on Wilshire. I've brought some of his cards."

Everyone reaches forward.

Except me.

I mean, I know I'm in the midst of an early midlife crisis. I know I'm confused about my identity as an Artist, as a Woman, as a Person. But one thing I'm absolutely clear about. *I will never stoop to cosmetic surgery.*

"Sandra?" Diane asks, jiggling the last card. "Dr. Gleiberman— he does laser eye stuff, too."

Whatever. To forestall further discussion, I pocket the card.

Meanwhile, my friend Alicia rattles on, forget collagen! What she's been getting are botox injections—just little ones, in the cleft between the eyebrows. It's improved her face, and improved her life. Not only has Alicia's frown line gone away, she says she actually *feels* happier because even while sitting on the 405, sipping hot coffee, or squinting into the smog, her forehead just *will* not make a frowning motion.

Serene, content, spilling her coffee with nary a blink, Alicia went and interviewed Marilu Henner for *InStyle* at a book signing and Marilu looked *amazing*.

"Older than me," Alicia swears, "and no under-eye bags. Totally natural, Marilu says—because she has those deep-set Polish eyes."

"No Eye Bags at all?" Diane queries.

"None," says Alicia.

"I'll bet you wish you had *those* genes!" Diane erupts, nudging me.

My bowels turn to ice.

"Oh, Sandra's Eye Bags aren't *that* bad!" Alicia interrupts much too protestingly, much too loudly. . . .

4. The Big-Bosomed Eye Bag

Okay. Obviously, I have the hugest Eye Bags in the world. Especially, apparently, when put side by side with Marilu Henner's. (It's funny—until this point, I hadn't even realized that, as women, our under-eye bags were being measured in formal competition. "Marilu Henner: the *least* under-eye bags we've ever seen." "Sandra? Wellll . . .")

Skimming *Allure* magazine in the grocery store one day, I see an article that mentions how on movie sets, when actors arrive in the morning with puffy eyes, makeup artists dab on Preparation H. Because what does Preparation H do? It shrinks tissue. It has to. Now. Because someone is screaming. It's a medical thing.

This news is utterly disgusting to me and yet, standing there in the supermarket aisle, it hits me. Given that I don't have three hundred bucks a pop for collagen or botox (mine is the five-dollar face-lift, the cutting of bangs), I'm thinking . . . *Preparation H could be the right beauty product for me.* Obviously, I've been wasting my time with Nivea moisturizer and Brian's L'Oreal eye cream, whose TV commercials show twenty-four-year-old models in gauzy dresses spinning dreamily through a field of flow-ers—all for a fourteen-dollar jar of pudding that basically leaves an oily sheen and your hound-dog eyes intact.

I mean, what woman over thirty wants a beauty product that is Gentle as a Summer's Day anymore? No: We want change that is epochal, cataclysmic, clang of trumpets! I didn't buy the Won-der Bra, I got the *Miracle* Bra! If they'd had the Four Horses of the Apocalypse Bra, even better!

And so, Preparation H! Why not? There are no false promises here, no vague, euphemistic talk about the seasons of a woman's life. No, it's: "Smear it on your rectum. Good luck." And you know what? It works. For two hours, I looked *amazing*—but by the end of the day my cheeks were kind of numb.

June 5

10:40 a.m.

●

Phone Call from Hollywood

●

A Sitcom Called *Me!*

The call is simple, immediate, direct.

Amelia.com is getting so many "hits" on my video recitation of "The Eye Bag Chronicles," Fox TV is interested in developing a show. Based on me—on my quirky, hip, hilarious take on the world. "They say bottle you and sell you, you—*you*—are a sitcom," Anita Banning, my editor from Amelia.com, enthuses. "They want to meet with you right away. You go in and pitch something as simple as 'a hip, neurotic thirtysomething woman living in the Valley,' and they're going to give you a deal."

Sitcoms? I've never given any thought to sitcoms.

So I spend a week studying some of the hot network prime-time shows, with their bright cheerful names . . . *Suddenly SUSAN! CAROLINE in the City! Everybody Loves RAYMOND!* And I see, as the week progresses, how this *could* be . . . the fulfillment of my Destiny. The surprise glowing center, so to speak, of my twisted life Maze.

Let's face it. I'm not an amazing literary mind like Joyce Carol Oates or, for that matter, a razor-sharp political mind like Eleanor Clift. Then again, nor am I a twenty-two-year-old swimsuit babe on *Baywatch*. No, this thing called SANDRA . . . lies somewhere in the middle. I've got an average body, an average mind—overall, I'm just an average person. But think about it! An average, middle-of-the-road person? That's the very heart of these TV comedy shows! (*Suddenly SUSAN! CAROLINE in the City! Everybody Loves RAYMOND!*)

Although it's true that the notion "This is about ME creating a bright new network comedy series, starring ME!" is a *little* over the top . . . Can it really be called hubris, in the classic sense? After all, being a sitcom star is the exact opposite of wanting to be, like, a *movie star*. None of us sensible adults over thirty fantasize about *that*. Having huge cameras examine one's pores microscopically, finding one's shaky footing before a phalanx of nasty *Globe* photographers while clad in nothing but spike heels and a tissuey size-two gown, helplessly watching one's grosses rise and fall as one is sucked inevitably toward forty, a future that only promises more and more plastic surgery because ticket sales from your latest action vehicle are down in Malaysia and Kuala Lumpur—

By contrast, having your own sitcom . . .

Take a moment.

Squint your eyes.

Envision the bouncy opening montage . . .

Of YOU getting into YOUR car with YOUR morning coffee, merging onto the freeway, hilariously spilling that coffee, to the studio audience's delighted laughter, and applause—

And this instantly appealing, down-to-earth Realness, it comes very easily to YOU because it's all just about YOU being YOU—not forcing it, just being very conversational—in a living room brightened by washed pine furniture and comfy Navajo blankets. Just like YOU would have . . . but a little nicer. On the first day, YOU might hesitate—but even that hiccup would draw laughter, and applause. Because YOUR vulnerability is OUR vulnerability, YOUR sayings are OURS, come December there YOU are saying "Happy Holidays" on the cover of *Parade* magazine.

Meanwhile, syndication checks are arriving at your house in such a deluge, the mailman is laughing—his head is shaking, he has his hands up, helpless to stop it.

Walk the path, Ruth said. Walk the path. What she didn't tell me is that this whole strange journey would lead to money, and fame.

. . . .

Having zero experience in the television field, I am given a crash course in sitcom "pitching" over the weekend by my new commandant—no other than my original mentor, fortyish, Jil Sander–clad, brunette crop-topped Amelia.com media buyer Denise Francis.

"So," I ask wonderingly, "literally all I have to say is that I'm thirty-six, neurotic, living in the Valley—"

"Why don't we be not quite so specific about the whole concept of age?" Denise cuts in, rapidly dipping her bag of chamomile tea. "Why don't we leave that open?" She smiles.

"Open," I say. "I like it!"

"And—not to say that we're not on terrific footing with Fox," she adds, firm as a schoolteacher, "but come Monday, when we go in to meet with the creative executives, we're going to have to carry in a little more *ammo.*"

My thoughts snap immediately back down to earth. The unspoken warning *here*, I'm gathering, is that waltzing in, throwing both arms out Liza Minnelli–style, and exclaiming, "This show is about ME . . . being ME!" is *not* how this business works.

Denise continues. A sitcom "pitch," she explains, is more than a one-line idea. It's a quartet, quintet, or sextet of characters who, if thrown together in a lifeboat, would all react in diametrically opposed ways. (She draws a pie chart: Spoked arrows representing diametrically opposed personalities leap, energetically, out of the pie. As though to certain, hilarious death.)

Because that is the essence of comedy, she says. Vivid, colorful characters. Grating on one another.

As Denise pushes on, I start to grasp what she is saying. Of course. Even a sitcom called *Carol* isn't just about "Carol." It's about Carol's struggles with . . . from out of nowhere, a phrase pops into my mind: "Her Slutty Best Friend!"

Or perhaps Carol might be . . . Forced to Begin a Law Partnership with Her Ex-Husband Whom She Totally Hates But with Whom She Has a Powerful Sexual Chemistry That Neither Can Deny! And maybe his name is Dennis . . . MacMillan. So the show is called . . . *MacMillan and Company. Or Carol and Dennis! Oil and Water! Opposites Attract!*

Suddenly a parade of vivid characters is conga-lining irrepressibly toward me, including a bossy mother-in-law played by a caftan-ed Shirley Bassey and wisecracking eleven-year-old blond twins. Obviously I cannot use these, because they are from other people's shows, other people's worlds entirely—

But I'm in the groove now. And so, over the next few hours, improvising back and forth, Denise and I flesh out a portrait of a neurotic ~~thirtysomething~~ irreverent/with a youthful attitude woman *named* Sandra, who, just like me, lives in the San Fernando Valley. She has this incredibly hip, dry sense of humor. Because neurotic obsession is the engine of comedy, we make a list of, yes, her quirky likes, her quirky dislikes, her "Foibles."

Sandra likes:

- Dogs
- Tylenol PMs
- Eating Koo Koo Roo chicken right over the sink ("That could be a funny scene," Denise says. "Think physical comedy. *I Love Lucy.*")

Sandra hates:

- Bargain health clubs
- "Funny" e-mail
- People with a lot of air miles

Also, Sandra is always on a diet. The funny Zone diet.

Once the "engine" of my comedy neurosis is humming, a train of hilariously bickering people start climbing aboard my sitcom as in a jaunty Western-era musical, waving frying pans, jabbing lawn implements. Spokes around the exploding comedic wheel of "Sandra" include . . .

- Bud, her eternally traveling musician husband
- Maribeth, her amusingly problematic officemate (at Sandra's fictional office, because you can't have just a lonely writer who lives by herself, not unless that sitcom is set in New York, where people are continually running into one another on bustling streets)

- Lenny, her amusingly "organic" ex-boyfriend, who keeps falling off his own yoga pillow

All well and good, Denise cautions. But at the *end* of the pitch, to really sell it, I'm going to have to leave the executives at Fox with a *warm* feeling. A warm feeling encompassed by the show's overarching theme. Something like: We all have Problems, but we also have Friends. Or, All of us Struggle, but we also have Victories. Or, Yes, we're all Human, but each in his own way is a Winner.

....

A reception line of youthful, relaxed-looking people in linen jackets and soft-colored ties greet Denise and me on Monday, four P.M., at the 20th Century-Fox studios, on Pico and Motor.

I expect the executives to be somehow grim and foreboding, like judge and jury, but they are not. Warmly they introduce themselves: Jennifer the VP, Stuart from Comedy, Mark from New Talent Development, Andrea King from Casting, and a thin young man in glasses simply known as Todd.

"Hello, hello," we all say, taking our seats on the couches, as democratic and evenly spaced as a television family.

It's impossible to tell who is the most important person here.

The only vital information one can gather regarding pecking order is that Todd is at the bottom. He has no last name, no title, and is fetching Evian bottles. However, when he's complimented on his tie, and begins to describe some troubles with his dry cleaner, the conversation comes to an abrupt halt.

Everyone turns, listens, nods, smiles, and then, finally, bursts into rallying cries of dismay and sympathetic laughter.

"You should tell that one to Leslie—what with all her dry-cleaning problems," Mark from New Talent Development says.

"Or Warren," says Stuart.

"Or Peter—"

"Sandra!" Jennifer suddenly exclaims, and I realize, in that moment, that Jennifer, tall and blond and easily laughing, is the person who hands out the sitcoms. I nervously finger my folder,

and the notes with my pitch (the characters, the lists of neu-
roses, the Ptolemaic wheels and spokes and dials of my rickety
comedic lifeboat).

"Let me say," Jennifer says, "on behalf of all of us, that we're
very glad you could come in today. We're huge fans of your
Amelia.com dispatches. And we *love* the fact that you live in the
Valley. You know what they say—the Valley is to Los Angeles as
New Jersey is to Manhattan." Jennifer pauses, grins, lets even a
little more light in. "You know, not many people know that *I* grew
up in the Valley—"

"What?" Mark says, leaning forward. "I don't know that."

"Uh-huh," Jennifer says. "There I was, a pimply teenager in
Encino, working at the Dunkin' Donuts. Can you imagine? *Me?* In
this little Dunkin' Donuts hat?"

A row of linen jackets crests forward in laughter.

Jennifer continues. "And . . . Taco Bell. Remember those old
Taco Bells with an actual bell you could—"

And now Jennifer is off and running on a series of amusing
reminiscences about her childhood Valley experiences.

At Minute Five (Jennifer gets fired from Frostie Freeze), I'm
thinking, Clearly they're in no hurry to grill me. They're in no
hurry to hear what I have to pitch. And . . .

Maybe that's a good sign! Maybe it means the deal is done,
mine for the taking! Maybe this meeting is just a chance for *me* to
get to know *them!*

At Minute Ten (Jennifer gets her first car—it's a clunker), I'm
thinking, more realistically: No. The deal can't be done. Rather,
this meeting is a test. It's obvious they know and love my material. But they're in the sitcom-producing *business.* And so, never
mind that pesky *pitching* exercise—the more crucial question
they're asking is, "Is Sandra a team player? Do we like her? Can
she relate to us? Is she good in a room?"

Energized by the thought that the grail is so close—it's right
there, within my grasp, I just have to close my fingers around it—
I decide, quite boldly, that I *am* good in a room. I join in the
laughter, leaning forward *farther* than Stuart, laugh *louder* than
Todd . . . great pealy bells of laughter. Sometimes, if there's a

paper's width of space, I might rush in a really fast zinger like, "Hello—it's just like the Captain and Tenille!" but I get out of the way quickly, tucking my legs into a barrel roll. . . .

Beyond Minute Fifteen (Jennifer gets measles or mono or something the night before the prom), I cannot remember who I am or why I came. All I know is that I am a hapless slave rowing, with the others, on the merciless Comedy Galley that is Jennifer. Dutifully cresting forward in laughter, then collapsing back on the couch with a "Whew" to wipe tears from my eyes, I glance at my watch for a quick "How're we doing?" and am stunned to see that Jennifer has been talking for *forty minutes*.

Denise Francis from Amelia.com clears her throat.

"Which reminds me of the pitch *Sandra* has been developing," Denise announces, nasally. "She's really eager for you all to hear it."

I am not, I think. I am not!

But it's too late.

Jennifer's face becomes somber—almost guilty, as though she has suffered some slight reprimand. She turns to me, her body language suddenly stiff. "Absolutely, Sandra. We'd love to hear it. Why don't you tell us—why don't you describe for us—how you see your character?"

Denise gives me a curt nod. It's show time.

I think of the dog-eared folder, the oft-thumbed lists, the many-spoked lifeboat, and I realize . . . this sitcom idea called *SANDRA is entirely too complicated to describe*.

And so (and for me, the moment is as dreamlike as though it were filmed in ABC Super Slo-Mo) I punt. . . .

I channel the "Eye Bags" essay. Which is to say that I turn to the ring of linen jackets and ("RUBBER TO THE ROAD!") do a rapid, hysterical . . . stream-of-consciousness regurgitation of previously performed material. It runs something like:

Blah blah blah blah EYE BAGS! Blah blah blah blah HAGGARD! Blah blah blah NICOLE KIDMAN! Blah blah blah PREPARATION H! Blah blah blah MIRACLE BRA! Blah blah blah FOUR HORSES OF THE APOCALYPSE BRA! Blah blah blah SMEAR IT ON YOUR RECTUM. AND HEY, GOOD LUCK!

The room shakes.

The room resounds.

Ear-piercing shrieks of hilarity cut the air. Linen jackets slump helpless over the sides of couches. Evian bottles topple. Tears are wiped. Noses honked. Kleenexes are crumpled, hurled. Clawed hands reach up, begging for mercy. Todd the Lesser is laughing so frantically, on one backward fling, he throws his neck so far back it actually cracks against the wall.

But still I—gladiator, omnipotent, blood-spattered, victorious—still I strain forward on my gilded chariot, lashing, cutting, hitting, panting horses' eyes bugging out as I whip them into an ever-higher comedic frenzy. And all at once, I feel . . . my hair . . . begin to move. It is swinging forward, back. Forward, back. Forward, back.

Swingy hair, I think. Swingy hair. And all at once I realize that . . . I am living it. Revlon Red! The Bijan moment! The joyous yawp! It is I who am six feet tall! It is I who wear the gold lamé pants! It is I for whom the trumpets call! It is I who am kicking through . . . life's thousand-foot Technicolor cyclorama!

"Oh my God," Jennifer says finally, when they can breathe no more. "That's enough. That's enough. Come to the party on Thursday, and we'll introduce you to Chris Freund."

Denise gives me a triumphant thumbs-up. The big guy. We've made it. We're in!

June 20

8:37 p.m.

Temperature: Hot hot hot

. . . and rising!

The White-Hot Center

of Beverly Hills

Industry Mixer

Cosmopolitan #1

The Miracle of Me stands, triumphant, in an elegant bistro, just off Sunset and La Cienega. I stand, like a Roman god, at the sparkling center of the world. Our glassed-in atrium is fringed by the victory decorations native to the area—small potted ficuses, twinkly white lights, peach tablecloths, and sparkling crystal goblets stuffed with upward-spuming napkins delicately curled as antique roses.

In my right hand, I hold a ruby-red Cosmopolitan in an icy conical glass so big if inverted it could be used as a hat for the Tin Woodman. I take a sip. So sweet. So tart. So perfect.

My new boss, Chris Freund of Fox, is talking. He is a friendly, unassuming, slightly balding man in khaki pants, flanked by a royal bevy of youthful assistants.

Ours is not like a boss/employee relationship at all.

Chris Freund chats in a warm, unguarded way about how he misses New York. "In fact, Sandra, I was surprised to learn that you *weren't* from New York. Your voice is so hip, urban, edgy, and irreverent."

"Thank you," I say. A canapé tray twirls by. Displayed are tiny, plump packages of lamb and feta. ("Eat!" Chris Freund urges me paternally. "Eat, eat, eat!" "What with the new show, I wouldn't want to be putting on *weight* at this point," I joke back.

"Oh, don't be ridiculous," he murmurs, patting my hand. "You look absolutely fine!")

From the next room come sounds of some sort of jazz combo warming up. In the warm glow of the Cosmopolitan, Chris Freund's words continue to float over me, to wash over me, to bathe me.

"As we begin the development process," he says, "I've just got a few quick ideas I'd like to run by you. But remember. It's your show. You're the boss. Feel free to say no."

"No?" I say broadly, feeling the alcohol charge me, burn through me like fire. "How about yes? Yes yes yes!"

He smiles, leans in.

"All right. I have this hilarious, I mean hilarious, young comic, she just killed at Toronto, who does this great monologue about the Safe Guy versus the Cool Guy. You know? It's the classic dilemma of a twenty-nine-year-old woman. . . . She's looking at turning thirty, she knows she should get married, but she's torn between settling for the Perfect Guy or taking a chance with the Fun Guy." Chris Freund is tickled by the memory. "What I love about Kelly's premise, especially as regards to a series, is that while it's hilarious, and completely fresh, it's still very rooted in reality."

"Absolutely," I, the Goddess of Hip, Funny Neurosis, agree. Even though privately I'm thinking, Never in my life have I met anyone with this particular romantic dilemma. Most of the women I know are happy to be with *any* guy, any guy who will agree to some sort of regular, reasonably monogamous dating schedule. If the fellow's cocktail of antidepressants aren't generating actual impotence, so much the better. But not to worry. I'm the boss. I can say no. I select another feta-and-lamb thing. And a mini-toast, with shrimp.

"I have another kid," Chris continues, "very hot, did some scripts last season for *Just Shoot Me.* Randy has this hilarious pilot idea about a twenty-five-year-old cartoonist in Chicago, like a John Cusack type but a little younger, who has a great career going but his love life is a wreck. Why? Because he just can't commit. It's called *Guy Bachelor* and it's a scream. You'd love it.

It's just your sense of humor. Very hip and edgy. Becky?" He turns to his assistant. "Be sure to messenger over—"

"Please do," I say.

Chris chuckles and adds, "Of course, there's a waitress who lives in Guy's building, Katie McNally, who's feisty, funny, and, unlike Guy, completely rooted in reality. Katie and Guy have this incredible sexual chemistry. Every time they're together sparks fly, but they can't help always being at each other's throats—"

As he continues to speak, I can't help thinking that again, in life, I have seen only the opposite. Two lonely, unattractive, *non-feisty* people who meet through Great Expectations or online, both desperate to have a relationship. They get along, their cats get along, but the sex itself is so disappointing that the two people spend most of their evenings sitting on opposite sides of the bed in their sweat socks, crying.

Is *now* the time to bring this up? I wonder. Later?

Chris Freund is on to a new pair of Talent.

"We've signed two girls up who we think would be terrific in a sitcom. They were teen Doublemint Twins, and all but in person, this is the key, they're absolutely down to earth. Because of that, I don't want this series to be too 'wacky' or too broad. Rather, I think the focus should be on their relationship to each other, to explore rich themes of friendship, and sisterhood. Let's pull the 'glamour' curtain back. Let's show these girls as not just models, but real people. Let's ask the question 'What's it like to be twenty-two years old, blond, gorgeous . . . identical twins?'"

Cosmopolitan #2

Chris Freund is still talking. The warmth of his voice is still utterly reassuring. But even swaddled cozily as I am in my Swingy Hair and my Yawp and my great, vast Victory Pelt, all at once, I feel it. The slightest little . . . Icy Stab.

I mean, yes, I'm having fun at this party, but I can't stop asking myself, Why is Chris Freund telling me all these stories? Why should I be concerned about all these feisty twenty-three-year-olds and their sexual chemistry and down-to-earth reality when what we really should be talking about is a sitcom set in the San Fernando Valley about ME! ME ME ME!

"It's just . . ." I suddenly find my voice. I try to match his casual, intimate tone. "Regarding those . . . Twins. Being in my sitcom? I'm just not sure twenty-two-year-old . . . models . . . know what it is . . . to have, you know . . ." I throw my arm wide for my patented Jo Anne Worley–esque kicker: "Eye Bags!"

"To have what?" Chris asks, putting a hand on my arm, smiling.

"Eye Bags!" I repeat, taking another sip of my Cosmopolitan. "Eye Bags. You know. That's my trademark. I'm all about Eye Bags."

"You are not!" he retorts, much too quickly. "What Eye Bags? I don't see any! You're a lovely, lovely person, Sandra. Don't put yourself down."

"Well, okay," I say . . . but like needles of hail, the little Icy Stabs are now coming thicker and faster. Does Chris Freund not know about my Eye Bags? Does Chris Freund not know about *the* Eye Bags? About their Hip, Urban, Irreverent appeal? Didn't Jennifer the VP brief him *about* the comedy "engine" (spokes exploding outward) called SANDRA? Has he not been updated re: the SANDRA project? Has he not been *pitched* . . . that thing . . . called SANDRA?

Apparently not, because for the past twenty minutes, we've been doing nothing but talking about that gal Kelly from Toronto, that kid Guy from *Just Shoot Me*, the Twins. . . .

I have this sudden realization that, like some mythical Greek figure, Chris Freund is a man who goes from meeting to meeting to meeting retelling the story he has most recently heard. But if so, I think quickly, cannily, maybe there's another hapless comedic entity coming up after *me*. And therefore, what I need to do now, in these precious few minutes, is to insert Myself and *My* Stories . . . into the Chris Freund chain. I need to get the comedic possibilities of SANDRA to take hold somewhere in his brain, like a virus, so he can pitch the wonder of ME at his next meeting. "At Fox, you know what we like to say—Everyone Loves

SANDRA!" he'll enthuse. "Do you know SANDRA? She's the one with the Koo Koo Roo Chicken! The Miracle Bra! The Eye Bags!"

Loudly—and somewhat drunkenly—rose napkins and crystal goblets and shiny silverware spinning around me like a roulette wheel, I start to pitch.

"It's like, why do we envy Marilu Henner's skin for looking so smooth and featureless?" I burst out. "What if the opposite were true—i.e., what if what was admired in L.A. was the ability to look really HAGGARD? What a sea change that would be in our town. We'd greet each other at lunch with: 'You're looking wonderfully HAGGARD!' Or, 'She's become so HAGGARD at 49, waiters flock around her like bees to honey.' Or, 'Your eyebrows are so woolly, you should be on the cover of *Vogue!*' Or, 'How do I get to look this FABULOUS? Coffee, vodka, cigarettes, and, of course, plenty of sun!' Then again, I can't take ALL the credit. I have to admit, some of it is genetic. By the time my Dad turned twenty-eight he had eyebags like Billy Joel."

But this go-round, it all fails to make sense. And instead of a slave-ring of linen jackets heaving forward and back, forward and back, in my own computer-generated Roman forum, Chris Freund is standing stiffly and wearing what I'd call an . . . Unhappy Face. It's this vague frown that says: "I'm not entirely certain, but I believe . . . you have turned my kidneys to ice."

"Preparation H," I plow on sloppily, trying not to slur my words. "It's like the Apocalypse! I mean, it's like forget the Miracle Bra, how about the Four Horses of the Apocalypse Bra? The Apocalypse Bra. Or you might say, 'Give me a kiss! I just turned forty, saw my own reflection, and decided: I'm going to change my name to Merle T. HAGGARD!' 'Cause you look so . . . HAGGARD—"

"What?" he queries, polite.

Cosmopolitan #3

Chris Freund has very much enjoyed our meeting, but now he has to go see someone named Jeffrey. Also someone named Skip. And Trish.

I have been left alone with the assistants, a veritable sea of

Oliver Peoples eyewear and spiked hair and chunky black plat-form shoes.

And more and more faces and mouths are talking around me, storytelling, narrating, describing, pitching. And as they are, the ages of the vibrant characters limbo-dancing through the *Manhattan co-op! Law firm in L.A.! Sports bar in Chicago!* keep skinching lower and lower and lower. No one in this room utters any words that begin with "thirty." No. We started the evening at twenty-nine, moved down to twenty-five, for a while we were at twenty-two, and now I'm hearing, "High school! They're like the hippest, smartest kids in high school! And the female lead is, like, eleven! You know, that awkward age where you know you should settle down with a steady boyfriend, but you can't decide whether to settle for the really Nice Guy or the really Fun Guy!"

Who do I know who's *eleven?* I think. Somebody's niece who lives in Boston.

Indeed, I reflect sadly, accidentally sloshing some Cosmopol-itan on my wrist and licking it off (no one seems to care—they're all busy pitching my ear off). Generally I find that people are a lot older in Life than they are in Television and the Movies. A parallel, invisible race—that's the rest of *us.* Padding about in our sweatpants, gray-faced, wanly pushing our carts through the grocery store of Life, eating Lay's potato chips right out of the bag as, unlike our bright, cheerful TV counterparts, we just keep getting older and older and older, year by year by year.

Not that real people don't have *similar* problems to ones characters have on TV. Real people, *too,* can't get a date, they, *too,* have hilariously humiliating jobs, but instead of being twenty-four, they're like forty-four. "I can't get a date and I'm forty-four!" I mean, look at Gwyneth (from Accounting)! She's having more sex than any other living human being and she's fifty-three! Fifty-three!

Cosmopolitan #4

Denise Francis, media consultant from Amelia.com, can't stop talking about how great the party is going, how great the deal is going, how great *we* are going. Denise and I sit together on a floral-patterned window bench. I notice, with a wave of weariness, that her thigh, in its black satin cigarette pant, is about half the size of mine.

"The great thing about Fox," she says, trembling with excitement, as though she is on speed. "The great thing about Chris Freund is that he is about development. He is about *supporting* Talent, about giving that Talent everything it needs, every step of the way. He says he's in this for the long haul."

The band in the next room has started to play. It's swing music, a festive melange of horns, and drums, and bass, and a laughing male singer crooning, "Jump and Jivin'! Jump and Jivin'!" And for the first time this evening, I feel a sudden familiarity, an ease, an unexpected lift of happiness from some long-forgotten place. "Jump and Jivin' "? I love that song! I think. I *love* it! Where do I know that song from?

And then I realize: *It's that Gap commercial!* I'm feeling nostalgic for *the good times I never had,* in that fictional *commercial,* swing-dancing with a bunch of laughing twenty-five-year-olds in Gap pants—aka pants, in reality, that I can't even get *into.* Nostalgia? What nostalgia? The only *actual* life memory Gap has given me is panicking in a Gap dressing room, realizing the only pants in the store that'll pull up over my hips are size REVERSE FIT. You know, for that "rare" woman whose butt is *bigger* than her waist—us *freaks!*

To my right side, Andrea from Casting is busy reassuring Denise and me about . . . some problem I was hitherto unaware of.

"I know what it seems like, reading the trades," Andrea is saying. "It seems like everywhere you look, twenty-four-year-old stand-up comics with five minutes of material—five minutes max—are being given million-dollar deals!"

To my left side, Mark from New Talent Development is agreeing with her.

"That's not what we do," he says. "What *we* do is take Hip, Edgy, Irreverent voices and we *grow* them."

"As long as they're FRESH and HIP and YOUNG—"

"And YOUNG and HIP and FRESH—"

What is this with these people and the word *fresh?* I think hysterically. The more they repeat that dreaded phrase, "Fresh YOUNG Talent," the more and more I feel like Haggard OLD Talent. . . .

And the more I feel like Haggard OLD Talent (age thirty-six— I should be shot!), the more this bitterness comes vomiting up, like raw sewage, toward all the FRESH YOUNG TALENTS at age twenty-four with their million-dollar deals and their HIPNESS and their FRESHNESS—

But look. Andrea's hand is on my right arm. Mark's hand is on my left. Every so often, they squeeze me, they pat me, loving, possessive. . . .

Which gives me another idea.

And that is . . .

Who's to *say* I'm not the . . . FRESH YOUNG TALENT they're talking about? Yes, I just turned thirty-six, but (thanks to Denise Francis's brilliant coaching) *Fox* doesn't know that. Indeed, how do they know I'm not, rather than an extremely well-rested (due to the miracle of the sleep mask) thirty-six-year-old, a FRESH (if somewhat tired) YOUNG TALENT of, say, twenty-eight—a twenty-eight-year-old who, hilariously, is a kind of insomniac? Because she's so neurotic . . . about her air miles!

How bad do my Eye Bags look today, anyway? Catching a pale, filmy reflection of myself in the glass, I feel like a yellowed—but wily old—cur. With mottled vampire teeth I can extend—or retract—at will. The debate racks me. Haggard or Fresh? Haggard or Fresh? As my executives speak, I continue to nod, unobstrusively . . . tilting my head over to the left, to catch less of the track lighting from above and more of the shadows of the potted dwarf (dwarf! I didn't notice that before—are they really *dwarf?*) ficuses, so the Eye Bags are a tad more . . . camouflaged. I relax my features into less of a rictus of desperate hilarity and more into an expression that is funny, and yet cheerful and winsome and . . . FRESH! FRESH FRESH FRESH FRESH FRESH!

"That Kelly from the Toronto Comedy Festival," Andrea

is agreeing with Mark. "Fox is very high on her. I think she'd be great as the lead in Sandra's sitcom. She's like a young Meg Ryan."

And in that moment, any last vestige of Denial vaporizes, and I know.

That's what "You, you are a sitcom!" means. It means "You're such a hip, urban, edgy, irreverent *person,* you could write jokes for a hilarious sitcom based on *my* life starring the adorable Meg Ryan! (Except ten years younger)."

"Absolutely," I agree, tossing my head boldly. "A young Meg Ryan. Sure!"

Cosmplta&*@n #5

I stumble out onto the patio. Bracing myself with one arm, I look up into the cool night air. I consider the Bermuda triangle the small, foul dinghy called *Sandra* is capsized in, the Bermuda triangle that is Santa Monica, Doheny, and Robertson, three or four or five avenues of boutiques colliding in an illogical V that is less a regular, functional throughway than a kind of Eurotrash *bikini bottom* of an intersection, some little three-hundred-dollar thing a sixteen-year-old would just wear once and throw away. . . .

And, looking up La Cienega, I see a flash of something large and white and frightening. It is a brightly lit-up billboard advertising a HEAD. This HEAD. The BIG . . . SCARY . . . PERPETU-ALLY LAUGHING HEAD that is . . . *THE KING OF QUEENS!* He *is* the king! He *is* the king! THE KING OF QUEENS is so massive and larval and so full of garish, explosive merriment—his teeth alone are like ten feet high—that I open my mouth in a silent scream!

I flash, at that moment, on *Fellini Satyricon,* where Rome is corrupt and foul and rotting and yet horsecarts keep rolling festively down boulevards with big god heads or, in the case of Fellini's *Amarcord,* big Mussolini heads, and I'm thinking instead of big Mussolini heads on La Cienega Boulevard this is what we have . . . THE KING OF QUEENS!

And just beyond, on the great illuminated stage of the next billboard, is Teri Hatcher. In *Cabaret*. "Teri Hatcher!" The name clangs through my head like a jingle ("Bu-u-u-uy Mennen!"). "Teri Hatcher. Te-ri . . . Hatcher!"

Why Teri Hatcher? I wonder, with a profound sense of tragedy. And why *Cabaret*?

I mean, in New York, *Cabaret* starred Tony Award—winning Natasha Richardson. In L.A.: *Teri Hatcher*. What happened there? Couldn't Natasha come do it out here? Was she not offered the booking? Did some linen-clad Beverly Hills agent say, "Oh no, forget Natasha Richardson. L.A.—that's Teri Hatcher country"?

"Te-ri . . . Hatcher!" Why is it every time I hear those syllables I feel like a kicked bunny, about to cry? Because—here you go! "Teri Hatcher" sounds like the name of *every mean girl* in junior high school, doesn't it? You begin with the kittenish, Southern California—sunny TERI (spelled T-E-R-I) . . . and then, just when you're struggling out of your too-tight bellbottoms into your size-fourteen bathing suit, out from behind the girls' lockers comes . . . HATCHER!!!

Interesting fact: At *my* junior high school, Malibu Park, right here in the L.A. basin, the sizes of the swimsuits we wore for gym practice were color-coded. You had orange, the petites; green, the very slim; red, the struggling with puberty; and then beyond, in no-man's-land, was whale-calf blue. You'd pull this thing up over yourself, open your fleshy arms wide, and say: "Citizens of Malibu Park? You may now begin *stoning* me."

And looking into the window, holding my fifth Cosmopolitan, ring of purple around my lips, dark canyons under my eyes, I see quite clearly that I look one thousand years old. Literally one thousand. I am like this dug-up semi-Asiatic Ice Age man who is walking through the alien planet of La Cienega as if in a dream.

The door bangs open.

It is comedy VP Jennifer. Jennifer the Valley Dweller. Jennifer the Dunkin' Donuts schlepper. Jennifer the Satanic Monologist. She has a hip young man in tow. They've come out here for a smoke.

I look at her and think: I can't hear one more story. I am a wrung-out shell. I have not one more drop of lifeblood to give to the Comedy Slave Galley.

I turn to run. But it is too late. She sees me.

"Hey!" Jennifer says. "It's our favorite comedy writer!"

"Michael Harris," the young man says, leaning forward, putting his hand out. "And you are—?"

"Thirty-six!" I shriek.

"What?" he says, still smiling. Other development kids are arriving, these . . . these identical *stick puppets* in Oliver Peoples glasses and Chinesey tops and chunky black platform shoes. Their shadows skinny, against the scrim of Mexican paver tile. Mine wide.

"Let me say it again," I say to the growing crowd. "I'm thirty-six! Thirty-six! Thirty-six! Thirty-six!" It's like I've been struck with this chronological Tourette's syndrome. Every time I repeat the number, I get this kind of self-destructive thrill. I imagine, each time, all these little Bridges of Opportunity being bombed: Thirty-six! Thirty-six! Thirty-six! Or perhaps I'm more like a renegade Buddhist monk setting himself on fire in a public place, as a kind of protest/performance-art piece. He lights a match; the watching crowd gasps; flames engulf him: thirty-six!

"That's right, Michael," I declare. "I'm out of the game. I can't be hired for anything. I'm as good as dead."

"You don't ever have to say your age," Jennifer says. "Although it's true, over at the WB, they say they don't want any writers over twenty-five."

"But I *want* to say my age, *Jennifer!*" Oh my God, I think. The Id! Breaking forth from its beastie-box! It's out! "Because I feel I *should* bomb these bridges, the ones to all that great . . . media and entertainment industry . . . *work* out there that is earmarked only for the Young and the . . . the . . . the fucking FRESH!

"Because you know what? I can't do it anyway! At heart, I'm old, I'm haggard, and I'm angry. As a matter of fact, *get to know me!* I've been like this all my life! Even when I was twenty I couldn't get with the . . . the Youth Program." I wave my arms wildly. "Youth seemed to be this dank pit (with Coors banners fluttering above) into which body after body was flung! Being Young was all standing around for hours and hours at dorm parties that smelled like vomit and Flock of Seagulls thumping and pock-marked beer kegs dispiritedly spurting foam like drool!

"I mean, I *could* do what everyone else in this wretched town does—pretend I'm twenty-six so I can get my next job creating the propaganda that makes our Young People feel that there is no escape from fetid blasts from the poophole of Spuds MacKenzie—but you know what? I don't *want* to be a card-carrying employee of the drecky evil Youth Culture mega DeathStar Spelling Hasselhoff corporation. (Which I think is on Wilshire, isn't it? That big glass building?)"

I am literally screaming at them. Spittle is flying. God, it feels good!

"Because I am *not* full of pep! I am *not* a character America loves. There *is* no Sprite in me. I would rather eat cold beans from a can—very likely what I'll be doing—than apply my few remaining brain cells to some already green-lit twentysomething romantic comedy where Jennifer Aniston goes on a hilarious blind date and has a mistaken identity mishap with—WHO CARES?"

And now, grandly, I pull myself taller and *curse them all.* I notice, on the Mexican paver tile, that now, instead of being merely wide, my shadow is looming vast and black and cavernous. My voice is a deafening harpy screech. My pudgy yellow talon stabs at them.

"And kids, wait till you get to be my age! Then you'll see how as the years go by, those birthdays just come faster and faster and faster! I swear, I had three new birthdays in 1998 alone! And you'll see how, after age thirty, each new birthday hits one like an accusation. With its disastrously higher number, each new birthday is a reminder of something you did wrong. You forgot to do your 'Stay Young' exercises, to take your 'Stay Young' pills! Because of this negligence, you're a year older. You've failed *again.* It's like: 'My God—is there some kind of migrant work crew I could have hired to keep this thing from growing over? They could have come the same day as the gardener and the pool guy. . . .'

"So all right already! Okay? I'm sorry! I'm sorry I forgot to stay young! If I hadn't been so distracted by life and work and whatever else, I'm sure I'd be twenty-six today. *Just like all of you!* But remember this one thing, you guys. Tempus fugit for everybody. Leo DiCaprio or no, you and I are on the *Titanic,* and we are . . . fucking . . . going down together!"

Later That Night

2:07 a.m.

Van Nuys,
Bedroom

●

A Dream

●

F R I E N D S

FADE IN: INT. SET OF TV SHOW *FRIENDS*,
CENTRAL PERK COFFEE HOUSE--DAY

The usual "Friends"--JOEY, MONICA, Ross,
Rachel, Chandler, and Phoebe--flop on
couches.

                    JOEY
It's like DATING LANGUAGE, you know?
"It's not you" means "It IS you."

Shot of Ross laughing, as Studio Audience
erupts into laughter.

                    MONICA
Loosely translated, "We should do this
again" means "You will NEVER see me
naked."

Shot of Rachel laughing, as Studio Audience
explodes into even louder laughter.

We now notice a new, unfamiliar "Friend"
seated just behind the couches on a little
stool. It is SANDRA, hair cut in a brave if
not-quite-successful Jennifer Aniston 'do.

                    SANDRA
Yeah, and I love it how "I think we need
to spend some time APART" means "I've
booked a one-way ticket to Australia--
Have a nice life!"

A taut SILENCE falls over the *Friends* set.
There is no Studio Audience laughter. There
is no "Friends" laughter.

                    SANDRA
(smiling, a little louder) I said, "Yeah,
and I love it how . . ."

Subtly, the *Friends* cast members begin to
move away from Sandra.

                    COURTENEY COX
(quick, professional) Security.

Two NBC SECURITY GUARDS come in, take both
Sandra's arms, wrestle her to the ground.

We go WIDER to reveal the shocked Studio
Audience, on bleachers. A kindly Midwestern
lady tries to comfort a little girl, who
breaks into a WAIL. A phalanx of GAP SWING-
DANCERS BOOGIE in, form a circle around
Sandra, begin to manically KICK her with
their pointy Joan and David shoes.

Summer
Where We
Winter

The Next Morning

11:43 a.m.

Temperature: 96 degrees

Van Nuys,
Bedroom

●

Hangover

●

Idea for a book proposal:

SANDRA'S POWER OF NEGATIVE THINKING

Unleashing Your Inner Critic

Negative Thinking Emergency Kit
(airline-sized bottles of tequila)

Negative Thinkers in History

Whatever Happened to
Drinking and Smoking?

No, I Can't

There Are Too Many
Unemployed Artists Anyway

Can I Lose Weight,
Make a Million Dollars?
No

Negative Thinking Exercise:
Get Out All Your Old Jeans
and Try Them On

Same Day

Three and a Half Hours Later

Temperature: 1,000 degrees

Outside My Window,

Fruit Is Exploding

Van Nuys,

Home Office

●

```
TO:      Anita Banning
         Amelia.com
FROM:    Sandra
RE:      New Submission for "Foibles"
DATE:    June 21

Hi Anita,

Sorry I'm a little late on the Summer Beauty
column, couldn't quite get it going. Hope this
edition of "Foibles" will do in the meantime.

Best,

S
```

The Way of the Ear

Recently it was pointed out to me—in kind of a hurtful way, to be honest—that people in Los Angeles are aurally challenged. That is, at social events, we simply do not listen to others. We do not ask them questions about themselves; we do not nod attentively when they speak; really, if we were to examine ourselves, we would realize that we simply have no interest in others at all.

The criticism came from a denizen of San Francisco . . . which rankles a bit right there. In fact, let me be so bold as to say that after many visits, I've come to feel that San Francisco people listen to one another too *much*. What with the cappuccinos and the smugness and the flouncing and the book groups, in the end they have very little to say and should be punished for it. "Come to L.A.," I want to say, "where you will be good and ignored like you should be."

But I digress. The point is, yes, we do listen here in our smoggy basin. Perhaps it is not all the caring, giving, loving listening that is offered on the front porches of tiny Midwestern towns.

Perhaps much of it comes at a hefty price the unwitting Mr. Spalding Gray, monologist, will pay later. But that is the way of modern "listening"—otherwise known as *controlling the flow of one's inattention.* And there are at least ten ways we do this:

1. *"Pleasantly Playing Computer Solitaire While Trying Not to Make Too Much Noise Clicking the Mouse" Listening*
   Most Common Practitioners: People with Retired Older Relatives
   Nowadays, it is possible to perform various forms of Low-Impact listening via the telephone. The advent of technological advances such as computer games and online services (like ones that let you check stocks) have enabled Low-Impact listeners to endure family phone calls much longer than in the past. Dangers include mouse clicks, heavy typing, or a sudden loud buzzer that goes off when you have finished Boggle.

2. *"I Married a Nutcase" Listening*
   Most Common Practitioners: Every Human Couple
   One of the duties of being married seems to be running from room to room while your spouse lumbers heavily behind, raving in a wildly disorganized fashion about someone who slighted him or her at work that day. Your job is to provide a buffer so the loved one in question does not take this ridiculous monologue directly out into the world, where he or she will be humiliated. The upside is that you can often do laundry or watch CNN at the same time.

3. *"Defensive" Listening,* aka *"They're Mad at Me for Never Listening" Listening* or *"If I Don't Listen, I'll Pay for It Later" Listening*
   Most Common Practitioners: Every Human Couple, Feminist/Multicultural/Other Oppressed Peoples Encounter Groups

4. *"Making a Deposit for My Monologue to Come Later" Listening*
   Most Common Practitioners: People with Friends
   What is a friend? A friend is a person who joins with you in the Universal Listening Contract, to wit: "You sit through my Hour-Long Rambling Monologues About the Vague Problems

of Life, I sit through yours." But so often people violate that contract, don't they? They do *their* hour and then say: "What's going on with you? Oops! I'm late for a meeting!" That is why we kill.

But no. Sometimes when the contract is violated, we merely reevaluate at the end of the year, like a board of stockholders. As we write Christmas cards, we consider the bum portfolio that is the Satanically Self-Involved (SSI) friend. Sometimes we renew for one more year, in deference to past years of higher aural return, sometimes we do not.

5. *"Keeping One's Face Very Calm and Supportive While Secretly Waiting for Gristly Bits of Gossip to Drop from the Groaning Board of Personal Disarray"* Listening
    Most Common Practitioners: Women with Friends

    My SSI friend Martha, on the other hand, has no saving grace at all except the graphic tirades she goes into about her miserable sex life with her husband, Walter, an aggressive tennis-playing lawyer whom all of us hate. "We are having problems in bed," she'd sigh. *"Terrible* problems. He does a kind of weird *pinching* thing. And *giggles.* I told him it was a turnoff and he cried." Horrible story, yes, but somehow you cannot turn away.

6. *"Not in Tune with My Needs"* Listening
    Most Common Practitioners: Graduates of Twelve-Step Programs

    Here is the paradox. We all enjoy *delivering* Hour-Long Rambling Monologues About the Vague Problems of Life. At the same time, we do not want to think of ourselves as pathetic. Because they always say the wrong thing, "Not in Tune with My Needs" listeners have a knack for making that happen. Example:

    WHAT THEY SHOULD SAY: "And what do you think David's problem is, that he keeps picking on you? Maybe he's jealous—he seemed that way at the office party. Also, he's putting on weight."

    WHAT THEY DO SAY: "You're so insecure all the time! Maybe you need to *love* yourself a bit more, give yourself a big hug."

7. *"Watch How Well I Listen!"* Listening
    Most Common Practitioners: Women's Groups, Touchy-Feely
    Nineties Companies That Value "Human Process"
    Now they smile and administer the hug to you directly, and
    you feel ridiculous and full of shame.

8. *"This Information Will Be Used Against You Later in Your
    Performance Evaluation"* Listening
    Oops! What sometimes happens with 7.

9. *"Passive Aggressive"* Listening
    Most Common Practitioners: Those of Us Who Still Insist on
    Suffering Through L.A. Cocktail Parties
    Fact: No one at adult parties listens to anyone else anymore.
    There is an old, long-forgotten concept about conversation that
    relates to the concept of conversational flow, i.e., If you toss *me*
    the ball ("Do you really live in the Valley, Sandra?"), I promise you
    that I will take that ball, run with it exactly ten yards—no more,
    no less—climax my story, end with a laugh line, and then toss the
    ball back ("But how about you? Where do you live—Pasadena?").
    Then *you* take the ball, then *I* take the ball . . . This is what
    used to be called . . . the Art of Conversation.
    When were we allowed to diverge from this pattern? When
    were we allowed to take the ball and run with it ten yards, twenty
    yards, fifty yards . . . eventually leaving the stadium entirely, per-
    haps catching a bus, buying a soda, heading down Mexico Way?
    In only three instances I can think of:

    a. We have recently suffered the death of a close family
        member.
    b. We are a divine entity with a message of relative impor-
        tance: Jesus, the Pope, Dalai Lama, Burning Bush, etc.
    c. We have been clinically diagnosed as schizophrenic.

At the L.A. cocktail party, however, there's always that one
monologist who defies all accepted Western social norms. Sometimes it's the sharp-nosed blonde in plastic earrings, sometimes
the hairy pear-shaped guy in a shiny NBC jacket. Either way, the

story's always the same: He/she has been in L.A. just six months and has already landed a job scrubbing toilets on *Friends*! He/she can't stop talking about it!

Not that the career choice is pitiable. Indeed, such dogged, unattractive people seem to be the types who most often succeed in network television production. But if only they'd ask us about *us!* Questions like: "What is your name?" "Why are you here?" "What would *you* like to talk about?"

Toss the ball! you want to scream out. Toss the ball!

But you don't. Because, unlike a normal person, the Passive-Aggressive listener is somehow rooted to the spot, paralyzed by hostility. Her attention jumps off the hurtling train of the monologue, speeding alongside instead in her own pace car, counting conversational turnoff posts that whiz by ignored, marking each with the point of a tiny accusing finger and triumphal "Aha!" Not that I would know very much about this.

10. *"Active" Listening*
Most Common Practitioner: Leonard T. Freed

It turns out there's only one person on the planet who does Active Listening. He is Leonard T. Freed of Ventura, California. I have tested Len on many social occasions, sending over all the women who feel that *men never listen* to them. They all come back nodding, crushed, tears in their eyes: "He *does* listen . . . like a dream!" Currently we have Len Freed chained up in a basement in Van Nuys. Call us. Appointments are available.

The Armpit of July
Don't Even Know What
Time It Is Anymore
(So Much Sweat in My Eyes
I Can Barely Look Up)
Swamp Cooler Died

Van Nuys,
the Armpit of the Earth

•

Ruth is now incommunicado in Nepal

Result:

I've utterly given up on life as we know it

and am suffering from a stupendous case of

Writer's Block/Person Block/Life Block

the likes of which I've never before seen

•

FROM: Portia Skokal
TO: Sandra
RE: Changes at Amelia.com
DATE: July 5

Dear Sandra,

I'm very pleased to be your new editor at
Amelia.com, now that Anita Banning has been
transferred to our Japanese affiliate
Banzaifone.com (the Z! Network!).

I've reviewed the columns you've written for
us and enjoy your hip, urban, irreverent edge.
I should let you know, though, that there's an
editorial push for all our columnists to move
away from the anecdotal personal angle and more
toward a service and information angle. A big
part of Amelia.com's current mandate (since we
are a live website that's updated daily) is to
be extremely timely and stay on top of trends.

To that end, our advertisers are asking us to
do a special "Bridal" section, and as soon as
possible, we'd love a piece from you on the
subject of West Coast weddings. In terms of tone
and style, cast your mind to some of the fun,
upbeat, and yet irreverent pieces we see in
InStyle magazine (where I was an editor). For
a more localized example, let me refer you to
the June 9 posting on wacky California "animal"
weddings by humorist Carol Ann Marbles, called
"'I Do . . .' Said My Pot-Bellied Pig."

Here are some other story ideas for future
"Foibles." Note that these are suggestions only;
I welcome you to add your own spin:

*   We'd like to have you go ahead and write a
    short essay (750–1,000 words) on breast aug-
    mentation. We're looking for a first-person
    viewpoint of "boob jobs" and what they mean to
    you. How do you feel about your own breasts?
    What do breasts signify for you? What do they
    say about our culture? We think that your con-
    tribution as an Asian-American woman living
    in postmodern L.A. could bring an interesting
    perspective to the project.

* Enclosed please find "The Bridal Gallery."
  This is a quirky first-person essay about a
  successful but lonely bridal gown designer--
  like a Vera Wang type--who finds love in the
  wrong place when she falls for the groom of a
  woman whose gown she is designing. We love the
  "water, water everywhere, but not a drop to
  drink" qualities of the concept, but feel the
  writing is extremely weak. Perhaps you could
  rewrite this in your own unique voice (but
  remember to use the name "Paula").
* Prentice Hall Publishing is a new advertiser,
  and they want us to heavily promote the volume
  described by the following ad copy:

"How much time and effort do you spend writing a
letter expressing heartfelt thanks, a special
note offering congratulations, or a difficult
letter extending condolences to a loved one?

"It sometimes used to take me an hour or more to
write letters like these. That's why I treasure
my copy of *The Someone Cares Encyclopedia of
Letter Writing*.

"*The Someone Cares Encyclopedia of Letter Writing*
contains over 525 model letters you can copy 'as
is,' or customize by adding your own words that
let your true feelings and personality come
through. These are heartfelt, thoughtful letters
that you'll be proud to sign as your own!"

  Any thoughts? Ideas? (Remember that your spin
  on Prentice Hall needs to be *positive*.)

Finally, for many years I was an editor at *Cosmopolitan*, where in an effort to improve the quality of our freelancers' work we developed a list
of "Clichés We Don't Want to See." I find that
writers who sincerely wish to improve will find
these extremely helpful. Although we all hate to
hear it, I've noticed that you tend to be a little
sloppy with your writing--you depend heavily on
clichés (as well as a lot of excess *italics*).
The following partial list includes many repeat
offenders we saw at *Cosmo*--you might want to clip

it and Post-It it to the side of your computer
screen so you'll have it there as you write.

Clichés We Don't Want to See (from *Cosmopolitan*)

The rest is history
John loves hamburgers. <u>He is not alone.</u>
A whole other ballgame
Give the cold shoulder
Everything but the kitchen sink
Fly in the ointment
To the manner born
Hey as in but, "<u>Hey,</u> I'm not knocking short skirts"
Yummy
Goodies
Traipsing
You don't have to be a rocket scientist
You don't have to be a brain surgeon
Go figure!
Fly off the handle
Pull out all the stops
Two sides of one coin
Couch potato
Running on empty
Throw in the towel
Come hell or high water
Throwing the baby out with the bathwater
Lit up like a Christmas tree
A little bell went off
Pure as the driven snow
Ice maiden
When the chips are down
It isn't over till it's over
Alive and well and living in . . .
Roll over in his grave
Jump the gun
Roll with the punch
Catch as catch can
When push comes to shove
Talk your ear off
Chance of a lifetime
Once in a blue moon
When the going gets tough

Pick of the litter
Sadder but wiser
Bet your bottom dollar
A shoulder to cry on
Win hands down
Six of one, half a dozen of the other
Tried and true
Significant other
Skim the surface or scratch the surface
First the good news
I jumped at the chance
Younger than springtime
Big fish in a small pond
Green with envy
Bosom buddies
Chances are
Prince Charming
Mr. Wonderful
Tinseltown
Male chauvinist pig
In your face
Go with the flow
A perfect ten
The bottom line
A kernel of truth
Whopping raise
Experts agree
Quick on the draw
Far-flung places
Come on like gangbusters
Tip of the iceberg
Like a bat out of hell
Throw caution to the wind
Going for broke
Tiger in bed
Toss in the towel
Reduced to tears
Coming up roses
Ran the gamut from (blank to blank)
Looking to make a change ("looking to" is every-
    where these days and is grammatically incorrect--
    it should be "hoping to"--you look to a noun,
    not a verb)

```
FROM:    Portia Skokal
TO:      Sandra
DATE:    August 3
RE:      West Coast Weddings
```

Thank you for your mailing.

A Lexis search reveals that the "Ikea furniture" article you sent us is very similar--if not exactly the same as--an article you have already published in *Buzz* magazine, not one but several years ago.

I really must insist that you deliver us a "Wedding Styles of the West Coast" column that we requested within twenty-four hours. For style and tone, I refer you to the latest lead feature by Carol Ann Marbles.

```
TO:      Portia
FROM:    Sandra
RE:      Wedding Styles of the West Coast
DATE:    August 10
```

Portia,

Here is the West Coast Weddings piece.

I want to add that while I continue to be
thrilled with writing for Amelia.com, I BEG that
your editorial staff stop referring me to the
"humor" essays of Carol Ann Marbles, as I believe
she is the worst writer who ever walked the
planet, and if I ever wrote anything that could
be remotely compared to hers, I would put a gun
to my temple and cheerfully blow off my own head.

Respectfully,

S

~~P.S.I find it ironic that you felt moved to send
me *literary* guidelines from of all places *Cosmopolitan,* given that this is a "highbrow" tome
whose recent~~

~~I very much appreciate the tips about the clichés,
and will tack them to my~~

~~Certainly we can all improve as writers, and
therefore I should mention how grateful I am that~~

P.S.I find it ironic that you felt moved to send
me *literary* guidelines from of all places *Cosmopolitan,* given that this is a "highbrow" tome
whose recent cover lines have included: "Nails,
Nails, Nails!" "Spring: The Right to Bare Arms,"
"What Our Doctors Aren't Telling Us About Yeast
Infections," and "Big Breasts are Back IN!"

Eleventh-Hour Bride

● ●

Enough years have passed; the wounds have healed; I can finally talk about my wedding. My wedding, since you ask, was like the great sinking of the *Titanic*. Then again, I knew it would be. That's why I was engaged for, oh, seven years.

Note how I refer to "my" wedding as opposed to "our" wedding—as if this were some auto-inflicted act. It is. Indeed, as the well-over-thirty (read "old") bride (for which there should be some special niche publication: *Old Bride Magazine*) plans her special day, the groom becomes but an extraneous character, a rubber mascot-head, a blank screen upon which the ensuing drama of the bridal breakdown is to be shakily projected.

Sound ugly? Never mind. Postfeminist women still deserve that nuptial ballgown and tiara, even if it comes ten years late and we're feeling bloated. To this end, I offer these Eleventh-Hour Wedding Tips. That's right. While you should throw a big wedding, yes, I don't think you should spend more than two weeks planning it. Learn from my example. Two weeks is just long enough to complete the hysteria cycle without killing you both.

1. *Have the Wedding at Someone's House, Preferably Not Your Own.*
For the years 1990 through 1994, my dream was to get married on the cliffs of Big Sur—string quartet, sunset, strawberries, champagne. We'd put up our fifty closest friends at the picturesque Big Sur Inn for one magical, unforgettable weekend. I made one phone call, got a grasp on general price and feasibility, and fell into a depression for four years.

2. *Pick a Religion—Any Religion.*
Atheists and agnostics talk a good talk, but come weddin' time they're pretty much left high and dry. When my cousin got

married, his explicitly Christian service posited marriage as a three-fold braid: Husband, Wife, and Jesus. My sister and I first snickered—then sobered up upon pondering the alternatives. What would our three-fold braid be? You, Me, and My Therapist? You, Me, and VISA?

Bottom line: Make a big deal about going secular, and soon you'll find yourself lighting an aromatherapy candle, mumbling about some Great Spirit's circle of love, and feeling much more embarrassed than if you had a nice pastor there reciting Psalm 105.

3. *Don't Sweat the Guest List: You'll Screw It Up Anyway.*

(A) Are they friends from college? (B) Have they had you over for dinner in the last year? (C) Would they invite you to their wedding? If the answer to each of these questions is no, said L.A. couple is sure to be the most pissed at your not inviting them. "But when do we ever hear from them?" you ask the air. And then at three A.M., two months too late, the lovely gift basket they recently sent will rise in the dark like a ghost. You scream. And so you are doomed to wander in rumpled wedding gown, botched guest list trailing, forever lost in the Palace of Guilt with its many alcoves and cupolas.

4. *Two Weeks Before, Let Slip to a Few Female Acquaintances*
   That You Have Made No Calls Re: Caterer, Flowers,
   Decor, Etc.

Why? Because it's fun. "And what have you chosen for your wedding colors?" a distant (twice-married) female relative asked me mellifluously on a Sunday night thirteen days before ground zero. A howl of laughter, while a satisfying conversation-stopper, was not enough to fully articulate my position. I pressed on:

"Wedding *colors?* I'm a person who can barely dress myself in the morning. Ben and I are getting married because we love each other. We've got the paperwork, our friends are coming, we'll have a big meal. That's it. It will be simple. This is a formal commitment between two adults, not a prom. We're too old to care about stuff like flowers and decorations and tuxedos."

To which she repeated, with a kind of eerie calm: "Sandra? What have you chosen for your wedding colors?"

5. *Immediately Take 60 Percent of All Hysterical Female Advice Given.*

And now, of course, the descent into madness begins. Wedding colors? Who gives a flying fig about wedding colors! Not you. But should you? Are you missing out if you bypass the wedding colors? Will that make you less than female? Less than bridal? Less than married? Just generally . . . less?

Suddenly a girlish pang of hurt wells up, a forgotten bolus of need from adolescence. You sense, vaguely, your Adult Head denying your Bride Head something princesslike, magical. What, there's a multimillion-dollar bridal industry in this country and you are not included? Who do they think you are? Gertrude Stein wielding a gardening trowel? So what if you're in your mid-thirties! That's just six years older than twenty-nine! You're far from washed up. You want to live! It's your last chance!

6. *Bridal Salons: No.*

Your huge plastic Bride Head, all circuits sparking like in the Disney Electrical Parade, will now pull you into a bridal salon, eleven days before D-day. Suddenly the Kate Hepburn–esque white silk pantsuit that seemed so perfect is less than bridal, less than married, just generally . . . less.

You need the bridal white satin, tulle veil, rhinestone crust. Thousand-dollar dresses hang accusingly before you in plastic body bags, glinting bluish under the fluorescents. You shrug one on. You immediately see that these are duchess of Czechoslovakia dresses. And you're of sallow biracial descent. The vision you see swathed in beads before you suggests the cheery title "Communion Day in Little Tijuana!" You burst into tears.

7. *Rather Than Being Mere Food Service Workers, Caterers Are Sensitive, Misunderstood Artists Who Are Continually Being Oppressed by an Ugly, Boorish World. Fifty Dollars a Person for Papaya-Brie Quesadillas Is a Fabulous Deal.*

No. Put that phone down. You are hysterical. Have a smart, sensible friend discipline these people. Not the wedding colors one.

8. *No Matter What They Say, It Takes Stylists Thirteen and a Half Hours to Do Hair. "My Wedding Starts in Twenty-Five Minutes and It's Forty Minutes Away" Has No Impact on the La Cienega Salon Person.*
Trust me.

9. *Don't Kill Anyone at Your Wedding.*
"Can Ben turn on the Nintendo?" one hapless eight-year-old asked after I'd spent twenty minutes, hair and gown increasingly bedraggled, marshaling the crowd—which, thanks to the Palace of Guilt, had swollen to two hundred—for toasts. I'm told my lips pulled back into a *Hellraiser* mask: The child in question let out a scream of terror. (Note that I did not follow tip #1: Do not get married at your own house.)

10. *It Will End.*
The day after my wedding was the happiest of my whole life. Oh my God, I thought, I never have to get married again. Ben thought so, too. And so on that first day as husband and wife, we were in bliss.

Dear Sandra:

Portia Skokal has just promoted me to Senior Content Editor at Amelia.com. I will be overseeing the online magazine's redesign.

Your contract comes up for renewal in September. Regrettably, your column "Foibles" will not be continued.

Thank you very much for your interest in this publication.

Best,
Carol Ann Marbles
BFG Publications

August 27

●

Un-Hilarious Summer Movie

●

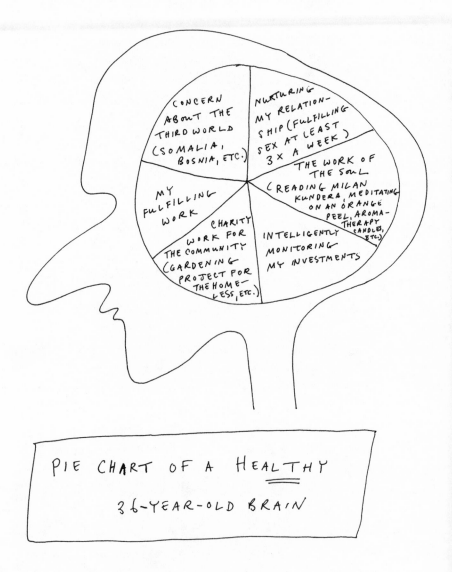

PIE CHART OF A HEALTHY
36-YEAR-OLD BRAIN

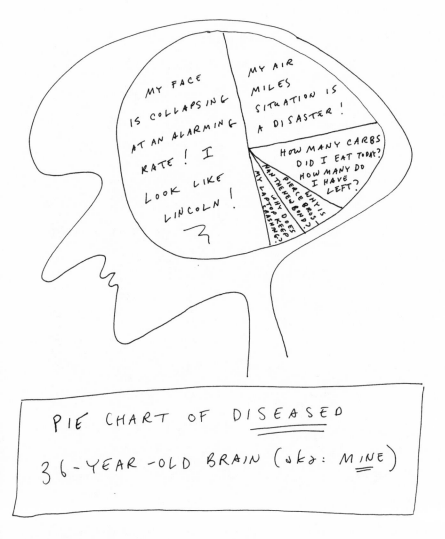

Eye Bags
The Final Meltdown

Driving to the tattered Wells Fargo bank on Van Nuys Boulevard to deposit my small, final Amelia.com severance check, I see a thousand-foot billboard above me of a laughing Mariah Carey. She has no Eye Bags.

Regis Philbin is also devoid of Eye Bags.

Even Wendy the Snapple Lady doesn't have Eye Bags.

I burst into tears in my car. I am the only person on the entire planet with Eye Bags.

Unlike Ruth said, there is no labyrinth.

There is no path.

There are no nano-particles.

There is only the Toad, crouching. And that is me.

And this particular Toad knows that, in a parallel universe, I would be thinking important thoughts and doing great deeds.

In a parallel universe, the story of my life would have Sweep.

In a parallel universe, I would be spinning important, gripping, dramatic tales—the types of narratives we hope to *see* in books.

Examples:

* Race to Antarctica, with only four huskies and a smallish loaf of hardtack
* Avalanche on Everest! Three anorectic male Palo Alto marathoners, no oxygen
* The Tumultuous Fight for Freedom in post-glasnost Berlin

161

Or even:

- Anna and Rick, a quietly doomed romance set against the sprawling backdrop of the Korean-American War
- Perverse Sex Among Twentysomething Heroin-Addicted Hustlers; Religious (mostly Catholic) Imagery comes into play via hallucinatory metaphors
- A Midwestern Farm, three daughters, tragic never-spoken-of history of Incest (an Oprah book?)

But no, this Toad is a product of a reasonably prosperous peacetime in a relatively comfortable nation. And as a result, a lot of pointless junk clutters up my head. Examples:

- What ever happened to the cast of *Grease*?
- "Cooking Scallops with Dom DeLuise"
- My shitty VISA card

Of course, in the meantime, I have this whole raft of major life FAILURES I *should* be meditating on: the collapse of my sitcom, the fucking-up of my column . . . the fact that *Barbara Kingsolver already* wrote *a novel about the Congo!* It's called *The Poisonwood Bible!* (How could I have *missed* this? How could I have *missed* this?) (It's because I've totally stopped *reading*. That's how worthless I am. I don't even *read* anymore.)

But no. I can't even do that.

In *this* universe—which is not Provence, which is not Tuscany, which is not the Congo, which is not even, as I've said, a nice part of Los Angeles—no, within *this* universe, this prison called Van Nuys, all I do is get up every morning and cry about my ever-crumbling face. I look in the mirror at my cavernous Eye Bags and feel helpless with sorrow. And utterly alone.

. . . .

But with that utterly alone feeling perhaps comes a kind of grandeur, I think the next day, with a new cup of coffee.

I mean, why are one's feelings about one's Eye Bags trite? Who said *the collapse of one's very physical self* is trite?

And indeed, in the midst of my glamorous aloneness, a new idea comes to me:

What if this Eye Bags thing were not some shallow, unmentionable neurosis to be swept under the carpet, but its own odd . . . heroic quest?

Let's say instead of small and uninteresting and dismissable and weak, I'm as much an outsider to society as . . . an ever-wary Sigourney Weaver. And (in deference to the summer blockbuster movie season), let's say these Eye Bag things are aliens. And if *Eye Bags I* was the road trip one and *Eye Bags II* was the light-comedy flop/misfire, this third episode will be the *final* and *most extreme* installment, aka *Eye Bags III: The Final Judgment*, or *Eye Bags III: The Final Armageddon*. (Tag line for the poster: "She's back—and she's not screwing around this time!")

Imagine the preamble.

(Picture the following in sci-fi vein, lines of text that spool slowly toward you from outer space. . . .)

The year is 2007, a couple of years after . . . the millennium. Our heroine . . . a kind of everywoman who represents, really, any woman over thirty who is watching her face collapse . . . Anyway, our heroine is drifting alone, out in space, far from the great mothership of . . . feminism.

Among the cold, cold stars, she ponders her lonely plight. Raised in the seventies, she'd always *thought* she was a feminist—that's what she was going to be when she grew up. But then, just the other year, like a bucketful of cold water, came that *Time* magazine cover. . . .

The headline: "Is Feminism Dead?"

Now, *that* wasn't so distressing. I mean, feminism is always dead, which is to say that it's always under attack, that's what makes it worth fighting for, women are a feisty people, hear us roar/blah blah blah/etc. etc. But what chilled her to the bone was the cover art underneath. Floating against black space were four ghostly heads, representing four phases of feminism: Susan B. Anthony, Betty Friedan, Gloria Steinem . . .

Ally McBeal.

Understand? It went directly from Gloria Steinem, sixty-five-ish?, to Ally McBeal, twenty-nine-ish?, with nothing in between! They skipped . . . a whole . . . generation.

And so, for our forty-ish everywoman, here's the conundrum. On the one hand, you lack the accomplishment, the legacy, the Nobel Prizes in Literature to run with the heroic Betty Friedan/Toni Morrison crowd, our tribal elders, wonderful shaggy white hair, tenty dresses, unretouched faces like proud battleships. But at the same time, your legs are way too fat to wear the miniskirts that all feisty young female trial lawyers do. . . .

See? That's the problem. Today's young feminists are supposed to be these waify little Riot Grrls! Grrrl Power! Spice Grrrls! They're all kick-boxing and snowboarding and spurning young hotties in Mountain Dew commercials and you're going, I'm almost forty! I look stupid in those barrettes! What's *my* answer?

COSMETIC SURGERY . . . is the answer for 80 percent of Los Angeles, but *my* tribe, well, we're just not cosmetic surgery people. We are the progressive-minded Sisters who've always gone dutch, saved the environment, believed that true beauty comes from within, "When I am an old woman I shall wear purple"/women unite/our bodies ourselves/etc. etc.

For us, cosmetic surgery has always been about a skeletal Helen Gurley Brown in capri pants, painted-on eyebrows all the way up to her bouffant hairline, tottering around Bloomingdale's at age seventy-nine a shattered woman in a size-two Chanel suit, squeezing perfume bottles with a spotted bony claw as she squawks at salesgirls in a single birdlike shriek.

Yes, that's the one thing we knew about ourselves: that cosmetic surgery . . . was the one thing . . . we'd never do. And certainly not as young as . . . thirty-six.

However, as one edges toward forty, and contemplates the genetic destiny *fate*—or in many cases, and thanks a lot, our *fathers*—have handed us . . . and one begins living, really *living,* day by day, the reality of Leonard Nimoy Eye Bags . . .

You start trying out, privately, to yourself, the *new* narratives that you hope might describe you in the second half of your life. Like:

"Um . . . I really admire Sandra's personal stand against cosmetic surgery. It's really inspiring that while everyone else in L.A. does it on their lunch break and looks great and throws it on the VISA and never even thinks twice about it, Sandra insists on aging naturally and now is so Haggard™ that she, um . . ."

"I think Sandra's Eye Bags are really beautiful and . . . and cool. . . ."

"*Her* Eye Bags are like these twin badges of wisdom! Uh, especially in that great *Newsweek* photo of her . . . accepting the Nobel Prize in Literature!"

See? The only appealing future I can imagine involving me *and* my Eye Bags necessarily hinges on my winning a Nobel Prize of some kind. It could be in Science, or better yet, Peace. . . . Because when I think of Eye Bags, and triumph, I think of . . . Henry Kissinger and Golda Meir. I mean, the only other professions I can think of where Eye Bags are an actual asset or, at the very least, *acceptable,* are like President of the United States and, um . . . Vulcan crew member on the *Starship Enterprise.* That's it! (Also, the late epic movie director John Huston. Have you seen his photos? We're talking Eye Bags *on top of* Eye Bags! Which is completely morally okay, of course, when you've . . . *won twelve Oscars* [another area, of course, of specific professional FAILURE].)

So this lost tribe I'm talking about . . .

Who are we?

We're not men. We're not women . . . because on Planet Earth the role of everywoman is always played by Michelle Pfeiffer, aka a person with absolutely zero resemblance to us. We're not the third sex, gay men. No, what we are is kind of a fourth sex, a mutant sex . . . females who faithfully go to step class three days a week, eat light, healthy meals, drink twelve glasses of water a day, and, at age thirty-four, look like Lincoln.

But are we sad about being so utterly hosed by genetics?

Surprisingly, no. Because remember, in this new sci-fi fantasy formulation, we mutants (aka fourth sex) are the rebels, the mavericks, the Eye Bags Liberation Front. There is a swaggering machismo, among us, as to who looks scarier in the morning. . . .

"You say you look like Lincoln?" I tell a compatriot the other day. "Thursday morning, I'm riding up a glass-walled elevator to a dentist appointment. And all at once I realize how every day, in every way, I'm coming more and more to resemble popular and much-beloved Asian television star . . . *Sammo Hung.*"

"Oh! Oh! Oh!" yells Jolene into the phone. "Have you seen me today? Catch me before four in the afternoon and *I look like Bert Lahr! I look like Bert Lahr!*"

Some would say this is a bad thing—but we do not. No, quite the opposite. We, the Prematurely Haggard Women, or the WWLLBL (Women Who Look Like Bert Lahr) . . . In our futuristic white caftans and robes in our parallel universe, odd *Logan's Run*–type bell clanging, we're trying to get in *touch* with our inner Bert Lahr. In our religion, Bert Lahr is sacred. Bert Lahr is holy.

And yet the invention of a secret new weapon—our very own light saber, if you will—gives us an option.

What is this weapon? The laser. The kind that can do laser surgery. Otherwise known as blepharoplasty—i.e., suckin' the fat out of the Eye Bags.

You're in and out in two hours. Three thousand bucks. American Express or VISA.

("Three thousand dollars!" Kaitlin exclaims. "Isn't there something else you can spend it on to feel more beautiful? A new hair-

cut, a new wardrobe, some, like, *fabulous* new shoes?" "Good idea,"
I say. "Then I'll look like *Lincoln* in a pair of *really great shoes*.")

And the more we study this weapon, the more we know it's
right for us. Because this weapon constitutes a major shift in
technology. This isn't *plastic* surgery, it's *laser* surgery. . . .

This is not your parents' Oldsmobile. These are, you know,
lasers. Modern. Clean. Bloodless. Laser/phaser. Laser/phaser.
Just like on the *Starship Enterprise*, they take this . . . this wand,
and they kind of . . . gently wave it over you. It's like . . . ions.
Molecules. Electrons or something.

Do you see the refreshing difference? While *plastic* surgery
has always sounded very Helen Gurley Brown in capri pants/
tottering around Bloomingdale's/bony claw/birdlike shriek/etc.
etc., *laser* surgery sounds very much like *us*. Like something
someone of our more youthful generation could do—and still
remain a part of our generation.

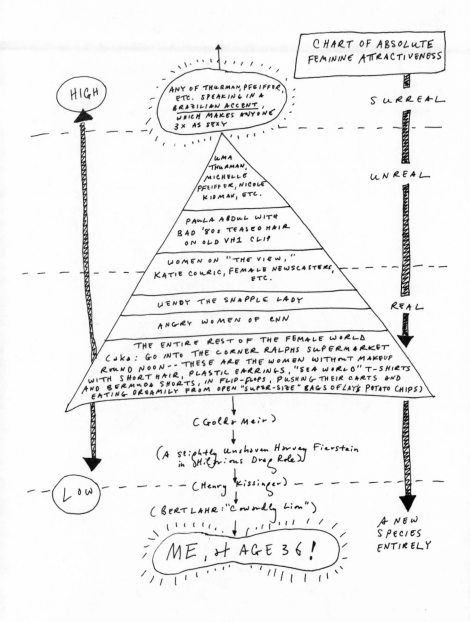

HIGH

CHART OF ABSOLUTE
FEMININE ATTRACTIVENESS

SURREAL

ANY OF THURMAN, PFEIFFER,
ETC. SPEAKING IN A
BRAZILIAN ACCENT,
WHICH MAKES ANYONE
3X AS SEXY

UNREAL

UMA
THURMAN,
MICHELLE
PFEIFFER, NICOLE
KIDMAN, ETC.

PAULA ABDUL WITH
BAD '80s TEASED HAIR
ON OLD VH1 CLIP

WOMEN ON "THE VIEW,"
KATIE COURIC, FEMALE NEWSCASTERS,
ETC.

REAL

WENDY THE SNAPPLE LADY

ANGRY WOMEN OF CNN

THE ENTIRE REST OF THE FEMALE WORLD
(aka: GO INTO THE CORNER RALPHS SUPERMARKET
ROUND NOON -- THESE ARE THE WOMEN WITHOUT MAKEUP
WITH SHORT HAIR, PLASTIC EARRINGS, "SEA WORLD" T-SHIRTS
AND BERMUDA SHORTS, IN FLIP-FLOPS, PUSHING THEIR CARTS AND
EATING DREAMILY FROM OPEN "SUPER-SIZE" BAGS OF LAY'S POTATO CHIPS)

(Golda Meir)

(A slightly Unshaven Harvey Fierstein
in Hilarious Drag Role)

(Henry Kissinger)

(BERT LAHR: "Cowardly Lion")

ME, AT AGE 36!

A NEW
SPECIES
ENTIRELY

LOW

OUR HERO

The ~~Dalai Lama~~

BERT LAHR

"THE KING OF EYE BAGS"

You know? It's like when you went to the health center in college, in the seventies or the eighties, and were told about the new STDs of *your* generation and they sounded immediately right. Syphilis, gonorrhea—that was *last* century.

"No, what people *your* age are getting is chlamydia, so here are some silicon pills."

My mind's made up. I dig out the dreaded business card. I'm booking an appointment with Dr. Howard Gleiberman, my magazine colleague Diane's Harvard-trained (did I mention that—*Harvard trained?*) ophthalmologist/laser eye surgeon on Wilshire.

. . . .

It is the morning of my permanent exile* from the tribe of Women of the Planet of Earth.

The morning of my permanent exile, my husband has just returned. He's finally back from the cruise.

This seems like a particularly terrible time for Ben to return, for my husband to see his wife in her most spiraled-down/failed sitcom/failed column/failed life/thirty-six-and-my-best-years-are-irrevocably-behind-me/Eye Bag Hell/Bert Lahr state.

But incredibly, Ben, my dearly beloved, who just a few months ago sprinted *toward* a van that was taking him away . . . Well, picking him up yesterday, I saw the same man sprint hysterically *toward* me and my waiting Honda. Clearly, time has transformed this "Jazz Cruise" of giddy high-fiving musicians into a kind of Das Boot tin coffin of taciturn monosyllabic strangers, richer, yes, but at the same time totally shattered by five straight months of playing Andrew Lloyd Webber.

Back in Van Nuys, Ben dropped his bags onto the floor of our

. . . .

*And I say this because, remember, in the Meg Ryan (aka culturally dominant) formulation of the world *(You've Got Mail)*, the heroine, Meg Ryan, is always timelessly cute *without* plastic surgery, while the annoying, evil, second banana, nasty, uptight/uptown Cruella De Vil–type person, played by a youthful Parker Posey . . . Well, the second banana *bad* brunette is the one obsessed with laser eye surgery. This is the subtle marker that tells us that any female type person who even contemplates laser surgery will *not* end up with Tom Hanks—i.e., *does not deserve love at all.*

cluttered living room, collapsed to his knees, kissed the rug. Then he slowly rose and, as if in a beautiful dream, began to wander about our ranch-style shack in a kind of stunned wonder. For the next few hours, he said very little. Contemplative as a monk, he watered the tomatoes, opened his mail, sorted his laundry, peed freely and lustily on his very own balding lawn.

"I can't believe I'm finally home," he'd murmur, about once an hour. "I'm finally home."

A more pressing issue: *Would* he drive me to my Eye Bag surgery?

He said he'd be delighted.

But, as I said, now it is the morning of my surgery . . . and I am full of misgivings.

Tearfully I ask Ben: "Tell me the truth, honey. Do you think I'm the most hideous of women? Do you think this whole project is ridiculous?"

Ben puts on what he has been calling his "strap-ons"—i.e., the *Cats* ears he had to wear every night on the ship, during the horrifyingly popular *Cats* medley. He points to them: "These, *these* are ridiculous. So what. You want to laze your Eye Bags. What the fuck. It's fine. You're lucky it's that simple. If I could wave a wand and have them put hair back on the top of my head, sweetie, I'd do it in a second."

And then he hugs me—not the Ideal Me, the person I wish I was, but the Real Me, flawed wreck that I am, that I've always been. And, in that moment, in that very moment, I know that I am loved. What a miracle. What an eleventh-hour gift. Worn, tattered patch of Van Nuys that I am, I guess Ben considers me part of his home, too. And home—the whole sum total of it—is what he has missed.

And with that, Ben goes to the kitchen to make us some French toast.

And watching his retreating figure, stunned by my good husband's essential patience, and sweetness, and kindness, it dawns on me that, fuck those joyless hags at Amelia.com, *this* is what marriage is about. It's not flowers and corsages and designers and gowns, it's about having a mate who will drive you—calmly, utterly without judgment—to your humiliating Eye Bag surgery. And who, beforehand, will make you some sunny, character-fortifying French toast.

Nonetheless, the next two hours are still two of the worst in my life. Getting ready for my surgery, I am struggling, in the presence of my beloved, to put up a brave front. I'm laboring to keep up that kind of savvy, that kind of quick-witted, that kind of hilarious Eve Arden je ne sais quoi about the thing. There is a spunky attitude, a winning self-deprecation, witty bon mots. I'm crossing things off my preop checklist, you know; I've got herbal medicines, ice packs, pillows, videos . . .

In preparation for the surgery, the checklist tells me to put on some comfy shoes, *check*, comfy clothing you don't have to pull over your head, *check*, and, of course, to shield oneself from the elements afterward—a broad-brimmed hat, "large-framed" sunglasses, and a scarf. . . .

Ben, who has been *so* loving every step of the way, so *gently* supportive, as though he's cradling the most fragile Fabergé egg of a person, goes into the closet and emerges, dutifully, with the only "broad-brimmed hat" we have in our entire household. His belated gift to me from Belize. An enormous, colorful South American I want to say almost like a *sombrero*. I fish through our bowl of leftover sunglasses, but the only pair I can find that aren't little "granny" glasses are these huge, octagonal, magenta-tinted ones from 1984 that make me look like a bisexual Beverly Hills Persian interior decorator named Baksneet.

Add a sporty floral scarf, an old Christmas gift of Auntie Ping's, and . . . You know? I look in the mirror and I see . . .

Joe Pesci in a hilarious summer movie involving funny mobsters and a wacky mix-up with a giant stuffed marlin at LAX.

I burst into tears.

Ben makes to put his Andrew Lloyd Webber *Cats* ears on again, thinks better of it. The moment's too grim.

And so my soul mate of twelve years and I drive, in sort of a shattering silence, to the white medical towers in West L.A. at like 100,000,000 Wilshire Blvd.—that veritable Sunset Strip of embarrassing medical procedures. And you know, it's eleven A.M.

on a Wednesday, high noon for the city's Eye Bags and chin bags and nose bags. All around, in the parking lot, in the elevator, you're seeing all these *other* slightly embarrassed people in hot-pink scarves and plastic $3.99 Thrifty sunglasses and Big 5 drawstring pants—

With a tremendous inner dignity, I enter the waiting room at Dr. Howard Gleiberman's and take my seat next to three other polite, professional-looking, thirtysomething people. We're careful to avoid one another's gazes. They are all studiously reading *Prevention* magazine, and they also *happen to have big Mexican hats sitting next to them on the banquettes.* It's clearly all any of us had in our houses. One of the hats has this jaunty striped sash drooping off it that exclaims: "Cabo!"

And, of course, just a moment ago, while walking in through the halls, I caught a whiff of ammonia. This has alerted me to the true reality of our situation, i.e., that we have all driven here this morning to be blinded, and die.

And in preparation, we've dressed for a cruise, and brought Mexican hats and snacks!

You know who we are? We're the Heaven's Gate people. With their Nikes, and hopeful bags of Chex Party Mix.

I mean, have we been sold any *less* a science fictive bill of goods?

"Yeah, man. It's called laser surgery. Thirty minutes or less, totally painless, you'll sleep right through it and afterward the bags'll be gone! You can go back to work the next day! The doctors, they wear tropical scrubs! And hand out these big green pills that are called Valium. They make you happy!"

But you know what? It was all true. Like a beautiful dream.

Furthermore, I can say without *any* hesitation that it was the happiest day of my life.

Of course, it's true I'd never had Valium before, and obviously, *that* is my drug.

September 14

7:06 p.m.

Temperature: A perfect 76 degrees

Hollywood, California:

Cahuenga Pass

●

Star Wars Night at the Bowl

●

The Gravy

When we yearn for things like VISA Platinum, we yearn for Rewards.

But here's the irony, I think to myself, as Ben, Kaitlin, and I roll down Cahuenga Boulevard in our (paid for) limo, to our (paid for) Hollywood Bowl box seats, where we will be dining on (paid for) Wolfgang Puck dinners.... (Our legs stretched out, the moonroof popped, a perfect Hollywood sunset stippling the rosy air above us ... !)

So often, the go-getters who actually *earn* the Rewards ...

Well, sadly, folks, they're so busy getting *ahead* in the corporate jobs that *keep* them in the corporate Platinum that actually *generates* the Rewards, they simply don't *have the time* to actually enjoy/languish in/sop up like flaccid, doughy beignets the swirly, oily Gravy they have generated!

"Indeed, thank God said go-getters have *us*—shlubs with no-Rewards lifestyles—to soak in all this ... this petroliferous Gravy *for* them!" I exclaim stoutly to my companions, sloshing more Taittinger (paid for) champagne into my glass. Because Kaitlin is the tap/spigot/flume, if you will, *of* this Gravy (her company has some client who is wooing some dot.com company whose twenty-three-year-old geniuses are working eighty hours a week on some extremely hot project for extremely hot people doing extremely hot things of extreme, extreme heat) ...

Because of that, I'm on my best behavior with my sister tonight.

And why not? I'm in a fabulous mood. The world is rosy-stippled around me, the Hollywood Hills are canons and fugues and rivers of rolling green, and I'm absolutely free, free, free of Eye Bags! More important, I'm free of worry . . . about the Eye Bags! The part of my brain that even *thinks* about Eye Bags? Totally (because it's been surgically) removed!

It doesn't hurt that, thanks to Dr. Howard Gleiberman, I've brought along a Jerry Bruckheimer–sized cache of high-grade postop Valium, which Ben, Kaitlin, and I have been liberally partaking of. Because it's taken in conjunction with the Taittinger, the three of us are fucking flying! (Brian, our fourth, is scheduled to meet us at the Bowl a bit later. Corporate lawyer that he is, the man has to work until eight. Poor thing. Coat-and-tie guy. Slaving away at the office, he's going to be late for the Gravy! Late for the Gravy!)

I reflect, aloud, on the nature of Gravy.

"Magazine Gravy," I announce, lifting my champagne flute in commemoration. "That's the best *I've* ever had. When I was at *Buzz*, it was all Aromatherapy of Rome candles, free facials, even a monthly lunch at Maple Drive. I'd *always* get the crab cakes with caviar. And I don't even *like* crab cakes. But when else was I going to eat them?"

"Dodger Stadium," Kaitlin offers. She's in a clingy white silk pajama outfit tonight that makes her look like the bestselling multimillionaire leader of some Malibu-yogic New Age order. "Have you ever been?"

Though a native of Los Angeles, I had to admit I hadn't.

"Before the ABC/Cap Cities merger," she muses, "where everything became one, thus effectively squirting *out* a lot of the Gravy, my boss's wife, Tessa, once gave my ex and me these special Disney seats right *on* the field . . . and we didn't even follow baseball! But the grass, the bleachers, the fading sun . . ." Her voice goes wistful. "It was beautiful." She turns to Ben. "How about you? What about musician Gravy? That must be something, huh?"

Ben utters a short bark of derision.

"Musicians don't *have* any Gravy," I correct her. "They live at the bottom of the world. You should see the buses they sleep on. And their health clinics! They're positively Dr. Zhivago–like, featuring fluorescent lighting and two-hour waiting periods among endless lines of Third World denizens."

"Our health insurance sucks because our union sucks," Ben says.

"Right," I agree, taking another sip of the excellent champoo. "Because *your* Local 47 officers are probably . . . ex-musicians themselves, you know, old guys from Frank Sinatra's day in smoking jackets who sit around all day saying, 'Fifty dollars? That's plenty for a casual! Back in my day we only made ten bucks and all the cocktails you could drink! Girls, too—we got girls!' They wouldn't know a good health policy if it hit them in the face."

"Not only *is* there no musician Gravy," Ben declares, a bit loudly, his cheeks flushing red (to match the tropical pattern on his Hawaiian-like shirt) with the outrage of it, "you don't even get the *steak* that comes with the Gravy! Even on the cruise we didn't get to order from that side of the menu! It was pasta or appetizer. Pasta or appetizer. On your fifteen-minute break. Then back to the Andrew Lloyd Webber."

"At our own wedding," I add, "Ben said to our guests, 'Will those of you who are musicians now form a line in the kitchen?' It was funny, kind of."

"Free saxophone reeds," he says, "*those* we have in droves. . . ."

"I'm serious, though." I turn to Kaitlin. "That health insurance thing is no joke. You know, Brian used to write me all these postcards from Europe describing, oh, the charm of buying gas in a Dutch-speaking country or trying to buy a typewriter in a small village in France. But I'm telling you—that's nothing compared to the white-water rafting adventure of getting a tooth capped in Van Nuys! For instance, last year, at my lowest point . . ."

I hesitate. This will definitely give Kaitlin more fuel for later attacks and phone conversations re: My Rotten Life.

On the other hand, it's such a great tale—like some ghost story. I drop my voice, dramatic. . . .

"At my lowest point," I continue, "I had to get a tooth re-capped at—are you ready? 'Dr. Campbell, the Credit Dentist.' You may have seen his ads on daytime TV. Or bus benches. His 'office' was in a tattered minimall on a garbage-strewn stretch of Victory Boulevard. In the sign, 'Dr. Campbell, the Credit Dentist,' I kid you not, the 'I' had fallen out of the word *Dentist*. It looked like a smile with a tooth broken out. No one inside spoke English except for one nervous white guy in a cheap (Ross for Less?) sports coat who kept looking over his shoulder as though expecting to be busted. At one point, large patient women from Third World countries readied me for X rays by gingerly laying over my body what appeared to be aluminum foil."

"Ugh!" Kaitlin's lean silk pajama–clad body shivers.

"Who needs to travel to foreign countries when no one speaks English in Van Nuys?" Ben calls out companionably, raising a glass.

And yet it's hard to complain about your lack of Gravy when you are smack in the middle of the Gravy Ocean. Fifteen minutes later, bathed in golden twilight, snug in the mini–pleasure vessel that is our Hollywood Bowl box, we are quaffing more alcohol and conversing, as we imagine successful media moguls might, as a white-shirted waiter brings pâté and arugula and tenderloin and filet and fresh-baked Tarte Tatin—all of which will be gloriously . . . written off!

And we notice, mingling in the concentric circles of boxes below us, glittering ghostly in white suits and white gowns, Panama hats over silver-gray hair, pale straps cutting across permanently tanned backs, holding their own sparkling flutes of champagne, are a vast array of seventies-era, B-level television celebrities . . . Susan Anton, Morgan Fairchild, Jim Nabors, more. They don't look tacky, though. On the contrary, they have a chiseled dignity—they look like regal elder members of some exotic animal kingdom with their huge manes of frosted silver, graceful in the yellow smoke of the fading sun.

It's a lovely sight . . . akin to the large balletic movements of brightly plumed birds at a watering hole at sunset.

In an odd way, I feel as if I've plunged through the *bolgias* of Dante's Inferno, squatted for a second in the Purgatorio, and have now been spit out at the concentric circles of the Paradiso—

aka the palatial Hollywood Bowl—everything glittering in perfect harmony, with its stately rings upon rings of lesser and lesser TV stars. . . .

"That's Los Angeles," Kaitlin notes drily as she surveys the scene before us. "A repository for used-up celebrities."

And, even through the gauzy haze of champagne and Valium and foie gras, once again, that old familiar irritation jabs me—the irritation at always being so fiercely judged by my older sister. Thirty pleasant minutes, and then everything always starts to go south. If it's not *me* being judged, it's my *city* being judged, or my *diet* being judged, or my *money* being judged. . . .

And I turn to Kaitlin, to flash a retort back, and see, to my surprise, that . . .

Kaitlin is completely focused on gnawing a chicken bone.

Her eyes are literally glazed over with the concentration of it.

She stops—just for a second—only to dislodge a piece that's stuck between her teeth.

And I realize, with a bit of a shock, that in that moment my sister is . . . *not thinking about me.*

That is, she threw out the comment about the celebrities and in a split second she has forgotten all about it and has gone back to her chicken. . . . *Do you understand how radical this is?*

The sentence clause "because Sandra is such an utter failure" was not even a part of her thought pattern! As opposed to how it usually is, e.g., "That's Los Angeles—a repository for used-up celebrities . . . *because Sandra is such an utter failure*" or "The sky is sure smoggy today . . . *because Sandra is such an utter failure*" or "I'm sorry that Adam Sandler's summer movie opened so much bigger than Meryl Streep's did . . . *because Sandra is such an utter failure.*"

Is Kaitlin, the Angel of Judgment, losing her edge? I wonder.

Or, God forbid . . . is it *I* who has been *imagining* things? Is it *I* who has been seeing the world through dung-colored glasses? (But can you blame me? I had Eye Bags! I *needed* . . . special glasses. . . .)

And if so, should I try to see things differently?

For instance, what if I take her statement not with the customary Sandra/failure filter over it, but at face value? Well, when I do, not only am I not offended, I actually kind of agree.

I begin a bold new experiment. I agree with a thing my pushy older sister said.

"Used-up celebrities in Los Angeles?" I say. "How about the Valley!"

"What do you mean the Valley?" Kaitlin asks, still gnawing on her chicken bone.

"Let me tell you," I rattle on, going a bit Jo Anne Worley with it, as I always do when I'm nervous. "There's no place for Weird Celebrity Sightings like the San Fernando Valley. Melrose, Benedict Canyon, Malibu: Forget it. It's all gated communities, industry pool parties, people putting their best front forward. But if you want to see celebrities being themselves, *Van Nuys* is the hotbed. If you're a celebrity who has either fallen so far—or, to put a positive spin on it, who is so comfortable with your own self-image—that you're living in Van Nuys, well, you just don't care who sees you!"

Ben nods in agreement. "Like at Nat's Early Bite."

"Nat's Early Bite!" I continue, emboldened. "Corner of Burbank and Hazeltine! It's regular people, it's tank tops, it's thong sandals, it's eggs, it's toast. A regular there? Ike Turner. Why? No one knows. But it feels right, doesn't it? You won't see Tina Turner breakfasting in Van Nuys, but you will see Ike."

"Here's another one for you," Ben puts in. "I just saw this one last week. Kind of a mystery one. At Art's Deli in Studio City: Paul Williams and Wilford Brimley. Together again. Why? Even more odd: They left in a light blue metallic Ford Taurus."

"The following week, a reprise of the theme," I add. "Paul Williams glimpsed at Petco. And then, two hours later, at Bed, Bath and Beyond."

"Paul Williams has gone crazy," Ben agrees. "Everywhere you look on Ventura: Paul Williams!"

"Paul Williams at Petco!" Kaitlin exclaims, clapping her perfectly manicured—if somewhat greasy—hands together with glee. "That's really quite funny!"

It *is* funny, I think. And as I do, this . . . this claw around my heart starts to loosen. . . .

Because before, mine seemed an all-celebrity world—ruled by famous people as titanic and powerful as gods—and I was nothing in it. Now, just for one heady minute, I'm at the center of my world, and celebrity heads are no more than Macy's Thanksgiving Day balloons parading distantly and benignly beyond. They merely decorate the world, like glittery wallpaper. And that's okay. That's okay. Why should it *not* be Matthew McConaughey's grinning mug looking up at one from the bottom of the shithill in the cat box? That's what's on magazine pages these days. What pictures would be preferable—ads for Sears mattress sales, photos of the horrors of Bosnia, leeches?

A Hopi-print chair rises before me, a tapestry of Balinese masks, the whoosh of the Pacific. I hear a distant clang of wind-chimes. . . .

And I think: Wallpaper! Wallpaper!

That's what Ruth was talking about!

I, the Toad . . .

Was looking at the hole in the cave . . . the television. A window onto a world . . . that didn't exist. The celebrity planet is just . . . wallpaper, i.e., not real. What's real is what's directly in *front* of me—this box, this wine, this food, these people.

That Ruth, I think, she's a genius. I'll be sure to tell her when I see her . . . in another four years.

We now welcome Brian, who arrives, slightly perspiring, in his corporatewear. "God!" he cries out. "What a day!" "Poor thing!" we exclaim, plying him with champagne, and Valium, and as we do, there's a sudden CRASH! Everyone's heads snap southward.

Just one ring below us, Sally Kirkland appears to have slipped in a champagne slick. A covey of white-coated Hollywood Bowl waiters fly to her side. Tottering about wildly in a fire-engine-red dress with matching fire-engine-red spike heels, unlike the other B-level celebrities in the box circle, she is *not* going so gracefully into that good night. . . .

"I'll tell you, I love Sally Kirkland's gumption," Brian

declares, nodding in her direction. "She gets that Best Actress Oscar nomination late in life. There's no way in hell she'll get one again. And yet you see Sally Kirkland at every Oscar show, and indeed, all around town, at every kind of glamorous function, head held high, brassy with cleavage, big hair, huge rhinestone earrings, always in red, telling the world, whether the E! Channel cameras record it or not, 'I AM HERE I AM HERE I AM HERE!' " He takes a slug of wine. "She's kind of a personal saint of mine."

"A personal saint?" I ask.

"Why not?" he replies, slightly defensive. "In her own way, she's an inspiration."

"So Brian," I say, trying to unravel his logic. "In your formulation—and bear with me, I've been doing a lot of thinking about this. . . . In your formulation, the Celebrity Planet is less Death Star and more like a kind of . . . Catholic Church, where we can adopt our favorite celebrities as personal household saints. Or an Ancient Egyptian religion . . ." I cast my mind back to the many hours spent watching A&E. "Where one can adopt one's favorite minor celebrities like special little cat gods—aka lovable household pets."

"Sure," he says. "While the media insists we worship the *newest* celebrities, the *hottest* celebrities, the *thinnest* celebrities, I've always preferred the ones who are a little off-kilter. . . ."

"Like MC Hammer!" I reply. "Going through thirty-three million in one year. Foolish but relatable. Who *wouldn't* want their own posse so much, they'd throw away their entire fortune?"

"You know," Brian admits, "I'd always thought dating a screenwriter would be like dating my own personal celebrity. I mean, when I first met Paulo, he was hot, hot, hot! Our first date was this big Hollywood movie premiere, for crying out loud! For a movie he got sole credit on. Sole credit! You know how hard that is? And, Oh my God, I'm thinking, I'm taking a rocket ship to the white-hot *center* to it all. Paulo and I are going to be standing, shoulder to shoulder, with all the stars, feasting and gorging—and then purging—ourselves at the glamour . . . trough!

"And so the studio says to him, 'Well, Paulo, you can sit way up in the balcony in the fuckin' nosebleed seats with your friends, or you can sit here, in the front row, next to, like, the star, Andie MacDowell.'

"And Paulo's telling me, 'Look. I love my friends to death, but fuck it. I'm getting them in for free, and anyway, how often do you get to go to your own movie premiere?' And basically it's the Elia Kazan moment where you abandon your friends . . . which people in L.A. do all the time because there are *never* enough party passes, you're *always* given just the one when you really need *three*, or *two* when you really need *four*, and by the way your group is complaining and by the way they're *dressed*—you said *formal* and the wife is wearing some kind of dubious *macramé* throw from *Target* that is going to get you *all* thrown out, even *with* the Miramax passes that are like hen's teeth to find, and you're thinking, *unlike* Private Ryan, these people need to be left *behind*—

"So Paulo and I get all dolled up in our tuxes and we *show* up to the opening and we *walk* down the red carpet. . . . And we feel like *glamorously dressed nobodies* because when we step out of the limo, because our faces are totally unknown, paparazzi actually *turn away from us* to reload!" Putting his arm up, Brian makes a stiff-backed, Martha Graham—like turning-away motion. "It's like a slap.

"Undaunted, we say fuck 'em and *take* our front-row seats, and when Paulo introduces himself as the screenwriter, Andie MacDowell politely says, 'Paulo who?' and we proceed to have a completely alienating experience a million miles away from his friends, from whom we are now separated by ropes and cones and barricades. It gets so bad we decide to bail out early but can't because we have to wait forty-five minutes in the underground parking garage for the valet parkers!"

"Oh!" all the rest of us cry out. Kaitlin pours Brian more champagne. I jiggle the Valium container. "Have another."

"Now you understand why Paulo and I have to flee the city as much as we do," Brian declares, tragic. "The farther the better. Forget Tuscany." He puts a fist up. "Next year: Australia!" He pops a Valium, continues. "So anyway, Story Number Two . . .

"Now, because Paulo's still such a hot ticket, we get invited to the Oscars and we're seated next to Joel Ferris at ICM, who has been handed, last minute, two extra tickets for the Governor's Ball. Whose tickets? *Madonna's.*"

We scream. Even my heterosexual husband, Ben, has managed a high-pitched shriek.

"And so we go, very excited, and I'm thinking that finally, this—*this* is going to be the glamour trough—the feasting, the gorging—we are headed into the very caramel center of the Madonna planet. . . .

"And—are you ready?"

We are.

"*Sitting at Madonna's table* . . . are a nice group of elderly helmet-hair couples who seem to be from, like, Viacom World-wide . . . Video Marketing . . . Textiles. In Houston. They are, literally, the most boring people on the face of the earth. They're so boring, even *they* can't remember who they are. Disappointed, I think, Maybe that's why Madonna gave this party the slip. She's already at the better party across town. The center, which is always somehow . . . one step beyond. In fact, I think on, maybe even Madonna is thinking to *herself* right now, 'Yes, I *am* Madonna. But I don't feel quite myself unless I'm with that kicky Sandra Bernhard . . . who's flying from New York right now . . . to Japan! For her little cabaret act. That sells so many less tickets than mine. And yet is in a way *so much more honest.*' "

"Right," I say. "L.A. being like this city of ever-narrowing concentric circles . . ."

"Concentric circles, yes," Brian agrees. "You get invited to Sundance, but not to the right parties. You get invited to the right parties, but your pass doesn't let you into the VIP room. You get into the VIP room, but you just missed Robert Redford by ten minutes. You get introduced to Robert Redford, but he's looking over your shoulder for someone else the whole time. Wherever you are, you always want to be somewhere else. Whatever you have, it's never enough."

"Maybe Los Angeles is all just . . . one big B-list," Kaitlin says.

"In a way," I muse, "the whole world is a Van Nuys."

"I think probably even Madonna has an inner Van Nuys,"

Brian says gravely. The thought seems poignant and somehow moving to him.

"Is there more foie?" Ben asks, his mind somewhere else entirely.

"You know what?" I declare suddenly, lifting my glass. "I'd like to make a toast!"

Obediently, everyone raises their glasses.

And as I look around at their wonderfully familiar, wonderfully flawed, wonderfully *life-sized* heads, turning maroon in the deepening twilight, I feel a surge of emotion coming on. The advent of a great Life Moment.

"Until this point," I tell them, "I've spent much of my life trying to achieve goals. Just recently, however, I've started trying to *abandon* goals. And I must say, to my surprise, it feels really, really good. In fact, it's kind of a relief."

"Relief," Kaitlin says. "That's *exactly* how I felt when my marriage finally collapsed!"

"Right," I say. "And so I'm thinking, maybe true happiness is achieved through maintaining a healthy goal-achievement to goal-abandonment ratio. Like a snake shedding its skin, every so often it's good to . . . to slough off one's 'success' personas, leave them behind. . . ."

I squint upward at the Hollywood Bowl cheap seats, on the high lawns. I imagine I can see long ant trails of faceless, transparent Ghost Selves—husks to be left behind—the Ghost Selves of all the botched, shattered lives of Los Angeles. . . .

And, in the cooling twilight air, I have this feeling of lightness, of airiness, of transparency, of buoyancy. I feel, in that moment, as though the balloon of my heart could rise, float over all these Ghost Selves of Los Angeles and forgive them their follies . . . and above all, forgive myself.

"Today," I announce, lifting my glass yet higher, "before all of you, I officially *leave behind* my . . . my Ghost Self of the Important Novelist. I boldly admit that I will never finish that Congo novel, I will never publish that Congo novel, in point of fact, I will probably never complete *any* novel." For Ben, Kaitlin, or even Brian to recoil in shock is probably beyond the realm of reasonable expectation at this point. Still, I'm glad I said it. "Hear, hear," they say dutifully, lifting their glasses.

Swept up in the moment, I go farther. "As of today, I also admit, before the world, that I am never, ever, ever . . . going to be a famous young writer. I'm never going to be a famous young commentator, a famous young comedienne. . . . As a matter of fact, I'm never going to be a famous young anything. Why? *Because I'm not young anymore!*" my voice swerves upward, in a sudden shriek. It's like a metaphysical alarm clock has finally gone off. The full shock of this thing is hitting me for the first time. I feel like I've been kicked in the stomach. I put a hand on Ben's arm.

"Oh my God," I gasp. "Oh my God, Ben. It's over. Do you realize that? My youth is over!"

Ben rubs my back. "I know, sweetie. But it's been over for a long time." I stare at him, horrified. He amends his statement. "What I mean is, even when you were young, so many eons ago, you weren't . . . really . . . happy." He sees *that* statement hasn't helped, either.

Hastily, he lifts his glass.

"Okay, okay," he says. "I'm with you. I think this is a good idea." He clears his throat. "Okay. Today *I* leave behind . . . Well, it's kind of silly to say, because it's clear I left everything behind a long time ago. . . ."

"You bet you did," Kaitlin says. "Look at that shirt."

"I got it in Caracas," he says. "Just eight dollars!"

"That much?"

"Anyway," he says, "for the sake of formality, let's say today I leave behind . . . my Ghost Self of the *Rolling Stone* Top Ten Major Label Recording Artist."

"For me," Brian says throatily, putting his hand over his heart. "For me, this whole Ghost Self issue is almost too painful to contemplate. Do we have ten hours? Is there a therapist on site?" He gives a bitter laugh, heaves a deep sigh, and adds, cryptically, "All I'll say is, things would have been much, much easier in my life if I had been born into the body of Jennifer Lopez."

"Not Meg Ryan?" I ask . . . but I know she holds no power over him.

"Except for the Oscar in documentary filmmaking," Kaitlin breaks in, "which my little sister says I don't deserve to win because I don't even know how to load film. . . ." She playfully kicks me under our little Hollywood Bowl card table. And the kick is hard, but it is familiar. And indeed, I think, as old ladies, Kaitlin will probably *still* be kicking me, ramming my wheelchair with hers, instigating unwanted interventions about the ramming, and blaming *me*. I'll always have Kaitlin, until the last step I take, like a stone in my shoe . . . and I guess there's some comfort in that.

"Except for that," Kaitlin breezes on, "I have to admit that my life is totally perfect and I wouldn't change a thing about it. I mean, face it, I've got a great job, I live in a great place—"

"Story Number Three," Brian says, taking her hand and grinning. "This is a nice one. . . ."

As the great Cinerama Dome of the world goes dark above us, Brian paints his final scene.

"So last weekend, Paulo and I go to this gorgeous wedding in Malibu, held at the Streisand Center for Conservancy Studies. Basically, this is a wedding at Barbra Streisand's old *house*, amidst Barbra Streisand's old *meadows*. . . . This is an enchanted, leaf-carpeted forest floor from which aged wood mini-chateaux raise shaggy, ivy-covered heads. It's not just the fairy tale–like buildings, but the fairy tale–like *vines* that caress the buildings, as though placed there by an ivy-*stylist*. It is *ex*-quisite.

"After savoring a salmon canapé rolled in pillow-soft phyllo, I duck into the rest room to wash my hands. I look in the mirror and see the face of a radiant fifteen-year-old. I kid you not. Gone is my pockmarked skin, my flabby chin, the crease in my forehead—gone, practically, are my nostrils. Gone. Under the welcoming orange glow, you can't even *find* a wrinkle.

"And suddenly my mind flies back to this gay luxury resort I once went to in the Carribbean. It was all about pampering. We were oiled, massaged, creamed, and wrapped for literally *days* at a time. It was a pleasure so intense I remember lying on my stomach, facedown in an aromatic lap robe, and thinking, I'd rather be old and rich than young and poor.

"At that moment, I turn and see a photo of the young Barbra Streisand—you know, forever nineteen—cuddled in the arms of the young Jon Peters, laughing. And I think, If this were a *Tales of the Crypt* and I could have any wish, however ill-fated, wouldn't I rather be *young* and rich? And I think, No. I'd still go with *old* and rich! When you're young . . ." He sighs, recovers. "You're still in the game, you have all these hopes and dreams, you're continually supplying sex for older people who aren't going to give you a job anyway. The hearts of twenty-five-year-olds are like clay pots shattered over a knee. . . .

"But what if you are a fabulous seventy-two with silver hair, swathed in linens, your battles *behind* you, and your awards *before?* Get in the car and drive to a meeting on Wilshire or Pico? Why? Sure, you might occasionally glide to the piano after dinner and hum a little something for Dominick Dunne, but that's about it. Further, since one of the most annoying things about aging are bitchy comments people make like 'God! You look HOR-rible!'— well, what if the only people you saw were a sensitive and loving staff? So even if your skin is lizardy, everyone says, 'You look great!' How are *you* going to know better? You're on pills!"

Ben says, "My theory? To Be an Artist . . . is to go through a series of psychotic episodes. You just have to make sure you're having the right ones in the right order. Reality sucks. A certain level of benign delusion is perfectly okay."

We finish the fourth bottle of Tatt's, the L.A. Phil starts playing, and to me, they have never sounded better. Even on the *Star Wars* theme—which, of course, the old me would have hated on principle, due to its grotesque tumescent popularity. But tonight I see it as just what it is—not the end of Western Civilization, but a giddy piece of fluff, a jingly sleigh ride, the sort of thing that would cause a person's whole body to light up, as if to say, "I've Got Mail! I've Got Mail!"

As fireworks explode above us, we sing along, the four of us, in our little Gravy box, the Bill Murray Lounge Cabaret version.

"Star . . . Wars!" POOSH!

"Nothin' but Star . . . Wars!" POOSH!

"If they weren't OUR Wars!" POOSH!

Blah blah blah blah!

STAR WARS, FIRECRACKERS, a HOLLYWOOD BOWL OF . . . OF NUTS . . .

The balloon of my heart floats high, high, high above our fetid—and yet starry—city.

What if this were the greatest place on earth? What if we were living in heaven and didn't know it?

Or maybe it's a delusion, I think.

But maybe we don't care.

Fall of Our

Dearest

Expectations

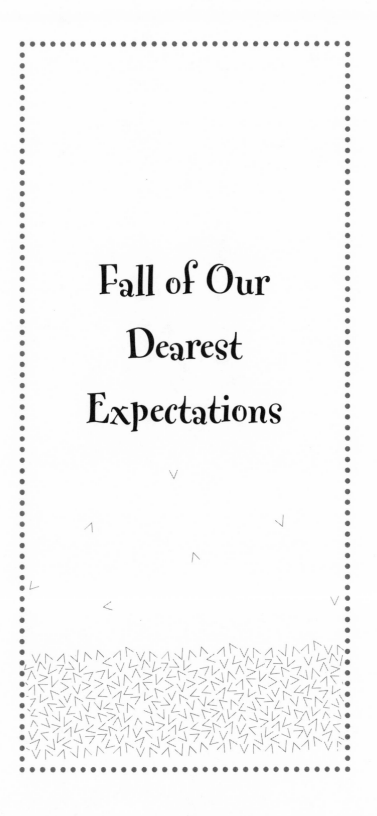

September 28

5:57 p.m.

Temperature: 68 degrees

June Lake, California

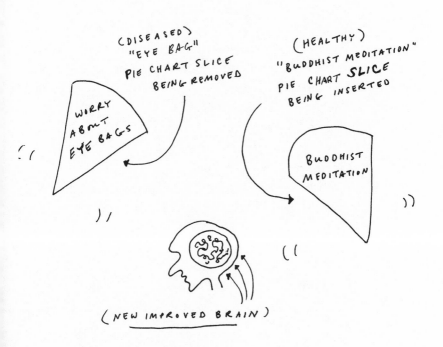

On the Road

The New Me
Ex–Congo Novelist
Ex–Award Winner
aka
A Buddhist *Par Excellence*
One of Our Nation's *Top-Flight* Buddhists
More Buddhist Than Thou

To commemorate release from my Any Life Ambitions Whatsoever, I have bought myself, as a gift, this book of 365
Buddhist reflections—kind of like your very own one-a-day cap-
sule of spiritual advice. I have been reading one a day, every
morning, during my fourth cup of decaf.

How's my foray into Buddhism Lite going? Well, so far every
saying seems to be about Letting Go, e.g.:

"You have an image of what happiness is . . . LET IT GO."

"In India, there is a story about a monkey clutching a juicy
mango in his paw . . . LET IT GO."

"Bodhidharma kept falling asleep when he was meditating on
a mountain top, so he tore off his own eyelids, flung them to the
ground, and . . . LET IT GO."

I'm finding the rhythm and feel of the Buddhist philosophy
very appealing. It makes me want to unbutton my own too-tight
jeans with a philosophical sigh and say, very wisely, "What can I
tell you? I have been clinging desperately to the notion of a
twenty-five-year-old body like a foolish monkey with a mango
in its paw. But now I have . . . LET IT GO. (Yes I *will* have
some pie.)"

So when Ben proposes—somewhat combatively—that we use this downtime, this free time, this unemployed time to take a week off and go camping, a proposal he has made every year of our twelve-year relationship, and which I've vetoed just as many times during said relationship, feeling camping and Ben and I will be a volatile combination . . .

Instead of arguing him out of it, I just serenely think: You have reservations about camping? LET THEM GO.

The tent, the sleeping bags, using the car window as a mirror while rubbing in Clinique Dramatically Different Moisturizer? Not obstacles, but wonderful Teaching Points.

Teaching Points for me and perhaps, ladies and gentlemen, a Teaching Point . . . for my husband.

Because frankly, for most of our marriage, I've been accused of being a person who could never take a vacation. No: "A picture of distraction," apparently, was I.

In my early freelance-writing years, Ben claimed you could never get me *away* from my desk, where I tended to wait, eyes wide, every tendon straining, for the phone *not* to ring. *Then,* once *on* actual vacation, I was apparently a person who was never . . . *in* the Moment. No, apparently I was the sort of person who was always bringing books and tapes and notebooks and laptops and other junk with which to *shield* myself from the Moment.

The theory was freely proffered that I was a person who *feared* the Moment.

And between you and me, maybe it's true. . . .

Because let's admit, in life as we know it, the Moment is often *much* less than advertised.

Waterskiing, for instance. This is not about waterskiing. It is taking a bumpy car ride to the dock to pick up gear. Strapping oneself into a smelly vest. Sitting on a bench near barrels of oil and gull poop, waiting for others to strap themselves into their vests, to make sure they get the really *good* vests, the really *snug* vests—

Do you know what I mean? It's never about the forty seconds of sheer terror while actually *on* the water skis.

The fact is, so *little* of life is actually spent in the Moment. No, most of the time we find ourselves dog-paddling through all the interstitial stuff *preparing* for the Moment. Because at its core, the human condition is not to *star* in the Moment, but to basically work in the *production* crew on the *set* of the *Moment*. You know? The sixty-second Thanksgiving toast will be performed at 8:33. But in the meantime, grocery bags need to be carried in, carrots peeled, water glasses filled. . . . All that enervating, lifeblood-draining *preparation* that makes one feel so much *less* alive than if one were slumped in a hammock with a vodka cranberry rereading *Valley of the Dolls.*

However, as I trundle ever deeper into the echoing canyons of my thirties, I feel a sea change coming on. I feel myself in the grip of a burnished new wisdom. I find myself more and more able to strip away the layers of fear . . . the fear of being bored.

Moment #1: The Sierras

It's exciting. Right now I'm *completely* In the Moment. Ben and I are standing, side by side, toes to the shore of a screamingly bright mountain lake, upon whose rippling azure surface a jagged, snowcapped range is reflected like glass in harsh glittery sunshine.

I *squint* my eyes, I *feel* the chill on my face, I excitedly *push back* the fake fur of my fluffy parka hood that's blowing forward into my face.

From the vast o-de-lay-hee-hoo of the mountains, a torrent of words, clear as a silver bell, starts Niagara-ing toward me.

"The Bear Tooth Mountains," I declaim suddenly, brilliantly, into the sharp silvery wind. "What I find interesting, Ben, is that, oh my God, they really *do* look like bear teeth. Look at that! See? Bear teeth! Isn't it amazing how in nature quite often things look *exactly* like their name? Whereas in Los Angeles, you get these places like Panorama City. Panorama City. Have you been there? It's like the opposite. But out here, it's like . . . the Tetons! Jackson Hole! Jackson Hole. I mean, descending from the air in a plane, it really *does* look like a hole."

"The reason I like to look at nature," Ben replies, evenly, "is because it reduces, you know, all that meaningless Monkey Brain chatter in my head."

"Oh," I say.

Moment #1A: or (Possible Reclassification) The Serenely Enlightened After-Moment

A shard of irritation toward my husband now presents itself. . . . I can feel my Monkey Brain rattling its cage—my Monkey Brain is itching to get out and start Spandau Ballet-ing through all the mind's nooks and crannies, upending paint pots, drawing nails across chalkboards, flushing already-overflowing toilets while screeching: I HATE HIM I HATE HIM I HATE HIM!

But then I think: LET IT GO. I take a deep Bodhisattvan breath and try to turn the problem another way.

I consider how the way Ben looks at nature and the way I look at nature are like two elegant (if, *yes*, mutually repellent) curves of a graceful yin-yang symbol! How grateful I am for this illumination!

Instead of flashing a curt remark back at him, I smile and impulsively take Ben's hand, squeeze it. I put a finger to my own lips, to indicate how crazy I am about silence. He gives me a wary look, like a bear being hunted. I smile even more, feeling smug. I'm starting to like this game!

~~Moment #2:~~ Ben's Father, Don, *Resists* a Moment

The second week of our trip involves driving to Arizona for Ben's annual family reunion. We'll be staying with Don and Dolores, Ben's retired seventysomething parents, in their smallish suburban house in Phoenix.

Length of stay: eight days.

SOME PEOPLE I know might panic. SOME PEOPLE I know might consider visiting their Elderly Relatives in Phoenix as possibly the most boring activity in the world, akin to watching paint dry. SOME PEOPLE might see it as a prison sentence. SOME

PEOPLE might fly into a frenzy of planning a rash of extraneous events to "break up," so to speak (and look at this violent language we use: "break up"), the eight days . . . of the family visit.

Look at Ben. With increasing panic, he is busily packing a sax, wads and wads of sheet music, a passel of funky old beach paperbacks, fishing lures, rubber waders, sunscreen, a Frisbee . . .

Poor thing. So frenetic. So frenzied. So *fearful*. Such a . . . dare I say it? Monkey Brain.

By contrast I, a kind of enigmatic Bodhisattva figure, I am walking the high-wire on this eight-day Family Growth Experience. I am not packing a laptop, I am not packing a book, I am not packing any magazines. I am not even packing a (crutch of the literati/crack cocaine of the chronically self-involved) Writing Journal.

"I say, Ben, if we're going to visit your parents, let's really *visit*," I tell my husband, giving him a pitying look as he throws what appears to be a yellowed copy of James Clavell's *Taipan* into a knapsack. "I say, let us use this as an exercise to focus our Monkey Brains on doing *one thing* at a time. Let's be really In the Moment. Let's really *connect* . . . on Don and Dolores's level."

"*Eight days* with my mother," he groans. "You don't understand. You've never spent eight days straight with her. This is not like listening to her on the phone and playing computer games. You're in the *same room* with her! You can't get away!"

"I'm not afraid," I say cheerfully. "I look *forward* to eight days with your mother." I take another Moment to add a zinger: "Next time you might want to think *twice* before saying a person is too 'distracted' to vacation."

So the first morning of our visit, here's what I do.

Empty of mind as a Buddhist monk (and temporarily as celibate, due to repellent yin-yang feel of marriage), I mount the stairs from our twin tiny trundle beds in the basement, the ones over which twin needlepoints of large-mouthed trout preside.

I pour myself a cup from the Mr. Coffee.

I pull up a stool to Don and Dolores's daisy-appliquéd kitchen counter, where Don sits quietly in golf pants, reading the paper.

I say, "Good morning!"

He nods pleasantly, looking up from his paper to acknowledge me. He immediately looks down again, continues reading.

I wait, smiling broadly, swollen as a tick with the energy of the Moment.

"Lovely day, isn't it?" I push on. "I love the weather here. So hot and yet so dry! I can see why you guys moved here."

Don looks back at me with the hunted bear expression that I'm starting to see is a trademark of the males in his clan.

The "Phoenix Life!" section of the paper is suddenly proffered. Don, I know, does tend to think of me as the Gal from the Big City, the one who needs to be immediately distracted with news of what movies are showing, what's on television, what pop music is number one. But all of that is in the past for me: It seems really quite Monkey Brain, I think, to gobble up news about Sandra Bullock's latest filmic foray when there is a living, breathing, incredibly special and unique Relative sitting but two feet away, a person one could be having Moments with right now!

But Don, I reflect philosophically, is obviously resisting our Moment.

Moment #3: Facing the Hydra (aka Ben's Mother)

The door bursts open. Ben's mother, Dolores, explodes into the kitchen. Her face is flushed. She is excited! She has been gardening! Her arms spill over with Bibb lettuces.

Now, as I've intimated, Ben has argued many, many times that his mother's conversation is illogical. (Which is why Ben cannot bear to listen to her for more than ten minutes.) (After that he starts screaming.) Ben's claim is that his mother tends to free-associate for extended periods of time (minutes, hours, days) without ever drifting within sight of a point.

It is true that, while I have a soft spot for Dolores (my fellow insomniac, my supplier of sleep masks), in the past, I have tended to—if not tune her out—engage her monologues with only part of my brain, the better to focus on sharpening my skills at computer Solitaire or Free Cell.

But today, I decide, I am going to do better. Today I am going to listen. Today I am going to be fully In the Moment, no matter how painful the effort of concentration.

And so, as Dolores jumps out the starting gate and tears into her monologue, I sit very still at the counter, cup of Folger's in hand, almost in kind of a yogi position, and I calmly—*consciously*—study the monologue's twists and turns as one would an elaborate dew-sparkled spiderweb in nature.

And as Dolores chatters on, for the first time, I start to see a self-reflective logic within her speech patterns that is actually rather beautiful and filigreed and ornate. After careful reflection, I realize that within the linguistic world of Dolores, there are three basic types of Conversational Logic Trees:

1. "I know a guy at the bank who says that he knows a gal with red hair who married a guy who used to have this cousin who moved to L.A. and plays in a band and works with a singer who says she knows . . . *you!*" That's the entire arc of the story. Someone knows someone who knows someone who knows . . . *you!*

2. "You say you've just bought a Volvo station wagon? This gal in our play group that meets on Sundays over beyond the school that's behind the church *also* used to drive a Volvo station wagon."

And then here the narrative can split one of two ways. . . .

Either (a) "And that gal seemed to love that Volvo station wagon. She was always raving about that Volvo station wagon. Said she never had any trouble with that Volvo station wagon." Or (b) "Had a lot of trouble with that Volvo station wagon. Apparently she had a lot of trouble getting foreign parts for that Volvo station wagon."

But now here comes the interesting junction in the road. Here is the logical connect that usually throws the distracted, impatient, unenlightened Monkey Brain visitor off the path, leading him to boredom, frustration, anger, taking a yin-yang symbol and breaking it over his knee, etc. Which is that, after another paragraph about the gal and her relationship to the Volvo station wagon, you *leap* from the gal at the school who used to drive the Volvo to talk about *any person* that gal knows and *any sort of problem* that person has.

For example, if the gal with the Volvo, etc., has a father-in-law who is said to have just survived a particularly grisly gall bladder operation, that can become the passionate new topic, carrying just as much weight as the original Volvo station wagon that, apparently, you drive.

3. "That gal's father-in-law had a gall bladder operation—isn't that what General Charles De Gaulle had? Or was that Maurice Chevalier? I thought with him it was a hernia. . . ." And from here we're on to the kidneys, livers, and spleens of the world . . . what Dear Abby describes as "the Organ Recital." This is a random free-for-all where one can jump from one organ to the next, and from one human on the planet to the next, since all humans have these organs, from Pol Pot to the checkout guy at the Hy-Vee to your great-grandmother on the Polish side to an unidentified person referred to simply as Hank.

See? If Dolores wrote the novel of her life, it wouldn't *be* a singular narrative about a singular person with a singular premise, setting, character arc, resolution, closure, etc. It would be more like . . . like fractals of stories or . . . or . . . NANO-PARTICLES.

Hm. Nano-particles.

Like Ruth said, there's a lot of energy in those nano-particles.

At any rate, *following* this mental flow chart, I find for the first time in my life that I am actually able to *converse* with Dolores. I've cracked the code! I've unlocked the secret! I'm *in* and *rolling* through her private nutty world!

"And then . . . *what* happened with the gall bladder operation of the father-in-law of the gal at the school with the Volvo?" I ask brightly, pouring myself another cup of Folger's. "Was it a Maurice Chevalier–type health deal or was it more like what happened with Hank? Or Pol Pot?"

IN-LAW CONVERSATIONAL LOGICS
EXPLAINED

ALMOST LIKE
FRACTALS

CONVERSATIONAL LOGIC TREE #1 :

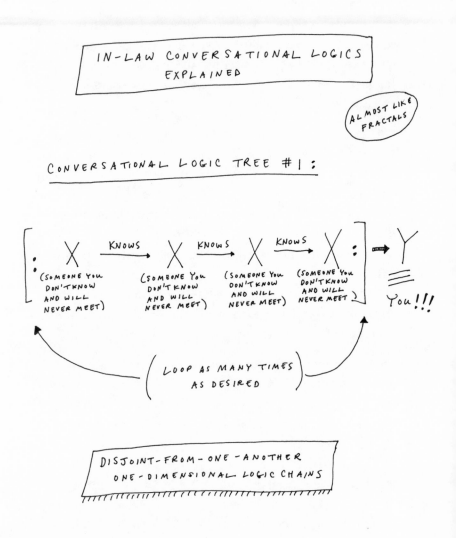

KNOWS   KNOWS   KNOWS

(SOMEONE YOU DON'T KNOW AND WILL NEVER MEET)

(SOMEONE YOU DON'T KNOW AND WILL NEVER MEET)

(SOMEONE YOU DON'T KNOW AND WILL NEVER MEET)

(SOMEONE YOU DON'T KNOW AND WILL NEVER MEET)

You !!!

(LOOP AS MANY TIMES AS DESIRED)

DISJOINT-FROM-ONE-ANOTHER
ONE-DIMENSIONAL LOGIC CHAINS

CONVERSATIONAL LOGIC TREE #2:

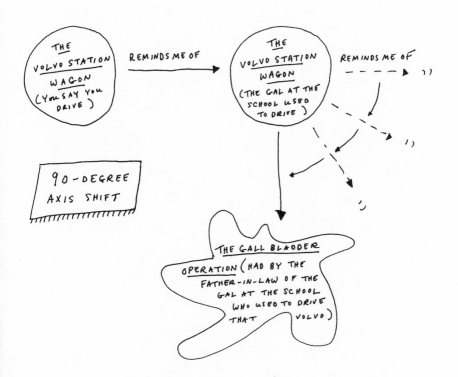

CONVERSATIONAL LOGIC TREE #3:

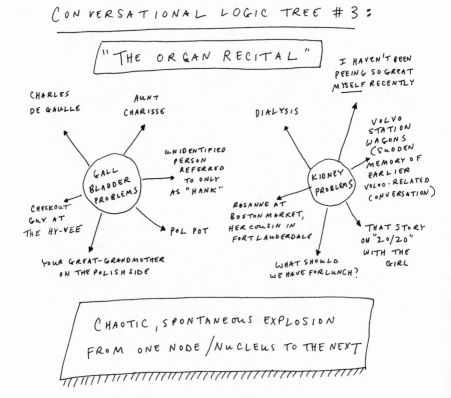

"THE ORGAN RECITAL"

I HAVEN'T BEEN PEEING SO GREAT MYSELF RECENTLY

CHARLES DE GAULLE

AUNT CHARISSE

DIALYSIS

VOLVO STATION WAGONS (SUDDEN MEMORY OF EARLIER VOLVO-RELATED CONVERSATION)

GALL BLADDER PROBLEMS

UNIDENTIFIED PERSON REFERRED TO ONLY AS "HANK"

KIDNEY PROBLEMS

CHECKOUT GUY AT THE HY-VEE

POL POT

ROSANNE AT BOSTON MARKET, HER COUSIN IN FORT LAUDERDALE

THAT STORY ON "20/20" WITH THE GIRL

YOUR GREAT-GRANDMOTHER ON THE POLISH SIDE

WHAT SHOULD WE HAVE FOR LUNCH?

CHAOTIC, SPONTANEOUS EXPLOSION FROM ONE NODE / NUCLEUS TO THE NEXT

"Something in between!" she exclaims, while Ben stares at us, haunted. (Don has gone into the bedroom to lie down.)

Moment #4: Ben Lowers Himself by Actually Speaking to His Wife

Now we get into Ben's minivan to drive back to L.A., and it's like the movie *Speed*, compared to Phoenix.

And here's the wonderful thing.

After staying with his parents for eight days, the formerly more Buddhist-than-thou, "Listen to that silence" Ben cannot have enough conversation. He is talking a mile a minute, he wants *me* to talk a mile a minute, and so now we're talking, talking, talking about anything and everything that comes to our minds.

We're babbling about how great Going on the Road is . . . and how all our lazy, collapsed friends in L.A. don't do it enough.

"Dennis," Ben says, referring to a forty-two-year-old bachelor guitarist friend of ours who lives alone in a crumbling three-bedroom in North Hollywood. Dennis is one of those bachelors who thinks a television schedule change is an urgent enough event to share with loved ones. Dennis is a Nosferatu with a remote control. Dennis will call you at 11:20 P.M. to say: "Hey! Did you see? They're rerunning that Jack the Ripper bio I was telling you about on A&E *right now!*"

"Dennis," I declare firmly. "Dennis is a guy who should move to New York. No, wait. Dennis is a guy who should live in New York with a *pet*—who requires walking. Between this trio of elements—Dennis, New York, pet—this would resemble a three-dimensional life."

"How about your friend Jolene?" Ben shoots back. "The Blocked Novelist/actress/lyricist/playwright/whatever. Maybe *she* should move to New York."

"Actually," I say, "Jolene originally *came* from New York—or perhaps the word is *fled.*"

"And now she lives in Santa Monica. Practically rent-free."

"Exactly. A musical based on Los Angeles bohemian life would be called not *Rent* but *Rent Control.*"

We think for a moment about Jolene, who's quirky and talented but who's starting to become hysterical now that she's fully in her forties and has no career of any kind. Clearly, New York—a place where quirky, talented, hysterical females are a dime a dozen, many of them with good jobs in publishing or associate editor of the *Paris Review* or something like that—was just too *rocky-shoaled* for her. But was L.A. a good fit, either? High off of a recent one-day UCLA Extension Seminar, Jolene has recently been nudging a cautious foot into comedy screenwriting, but with mixed results. It turns out Jolene communicates her wit through short winging bursts and then careens just as quickly off into murky bogs that feel like Despair. And here she is in L.A., where everyone thinks your work should be summed up in one sentence—L.A. being so, you know, *Ivan Reitman.*

"Austin!" I cry out. "That's the solution! Jolene could have some sort of quirky, charming, hard-to-pin-down column in the—do they have like an *LA Weekly* in Austin? An *Austin Weekly*? Tyah. There you go! It would be perfect. For each of us," I conclude grandly, "there is a dream city. And in that dream city, we are all free to paint our own paintings and sing our own songs and get our own groceries, or have them delivered."

We whiz by a sign that reads: SANTA FE—TURNPIKE 12 MILES BACK.

"Santa Fe," I say to Ben, chuckling. "Can you believe that at one point I wanted us to move to Santa Fe?"

What I don't say is, what I'm really holding out for is Oglala Springs—you know, that perfect little gem of a town that's gorgeous, and safe, and . . . and . . .

I look up into the blue, blue sky, that floating carnival of limitless desert clouds . . . and I think that we should keep on driving. We should keep on driving, driving, driving without ever going back. If we make a break for it now, we need never go back to Van Nuys, with its heat and its dirt and its tire shops. . . .

But Ben has just been telling me about how much he loves it—its very squalor, which is to say, its very cheapness.

"I can't go on another cruise," he has been telling me. "I can't play any more Andrew Lloyd Webber. Let's put the money I *made*

on the cruise *away*. Our expenses are *low* in the Valley. Don't you
see? If we stay put, stick with what we have, we won't have to
make huge amounts of money. We can be Artists. We can *control*
our time. We can be free."

Well, I don't know about *that*, I think. But it's true that, for
the Moment, our plans for the future can wait. For the Moment,
our next destination is nothing more dramatic than lunch. For
just these few miles and just these few minutes, we can . . .

LET IT GO, I think. LET IT GO.

And now, as the highway turns north, we start hurtling into
the great backlands of the middle desert. Looking directly into
the face of danger, I toss away our carefully cataloged cassette box
of culturally appropriate musics and throw our fate to the mercy
of the radio. . . .

And we're reminded that the spirit of the great vast West
will always sound like: "Screedle! Scruh-scruh screedle! Wao,
wao, wao."

It's "High Desert Rock! 84.7! Rockin' the Mojave!"

We cackle with surprise, and glee.

As Ben and I speed forward, the deejays continue to intone
magical names we haven't heard in years: Bad Company, Grand
Funk Railroad, Fog Hat. There's even Modern Rock: the Jethro
Tull song with the flutes, "Fuh fuh fuh, fuh fuh fuh, fuh fuh fuh,
fuh fuh fuh." And of course, eternally great, there's always Led
Zeppelin: "I'm gonna give you every inch of mah love!"

And Ben, in recovery from his Kenny G/"Smooth Jazz"/*Cats*
cruise life—Ben remembers playing in his first blues band in the
Midwest to "Rock the Prairie!" and he smiles.

As we whiz through barren desert, past a rusting mobile
home hunched on a pile of rocks under the rilled bloom of a
satellite dish, I initiate my favorite driving game—those wonderful old gedankenexperiments of the road.

For instance: "Where would be the worst place to live in the
entire Southwest?" Then I offer its corollary, "Where would be
the worst place to break down?"

Ben says: "Death Valley."

I agree, raising him one: "Death Valley, naked, no shoes."

I push on, invoking the classic "Devil's Postpile"/"Devil's Punch Bowl" question, i.e., "What is the worst 'Devil's Something' name you can think of?"

"The Devil's Shoehorn," Ben offers.

"How about the Devil's Toe-Clipper," I suggest, "or the Devil's Lint-Remover?"

"That's a good one," he humors me, and we speed on, happy ants—for the Moment—in that vast thing called the Great American West.

October 12

Temperature: 68 degrees

Snap of Fall in the Air,

Making One Think About

Going Back to School

Jolene's Bungalow,

Santa Monica

●

Meeting of Jolene's New "Right to Write" Group

●

Against Writing

It's a familiar narrative—rapid, raw, and confessional, with the usual half-bitten-off sentences, the usual dark stripe of guilt running through the center:

She's a marketing executive, fortyish, successful, but finding herself more and more bored with it. On a whim, she'd signed up for a fiction class at UCLA Extension. What few people from her "business" life know is that she used to love to write fiction in college, in her twenties, way back when! But then, of course, for some reason . . . (faint exhalation) . . . she stopped.

Anyway, she loved this class, loved the teacher, met some really great people, felt all fired up, started three short stories she was really excited about . . .

And now, six months later, she finds she can barely drag herself to the computer.

"I was so frustrated last night," she says as we all shift in our folding chairs. I check my watch. In forty minutes, lunch. I'll just have to sit tight until then, maintain an expression of patience.

"I was so frustrated last night," she says, "that I decided to start journaling *about* my frustration. I treat it like an exercise. 'Okay,' I ask myself, 'why do I have such a hard time just *sitting down and writing?*' I make a list."

The marketing executive ticks off the items on her fingers.

"(A) I hate the solitude of it. (B) When I'm at home, it seems like there are just a million things I'd rather be doing—cleaning the house, watching *Biography*, giving myself a pedicure!" Wry laughter, recovery. "(C) Every time I reread what I have, my inner critic turns on and I start feeling like maybe the idea of my story is not very good. . . ." Her eyes grow wide—there's moisture. Her voice drops.

"And then I start thinking about my Dad. . . ."

"The retired engineer?" Jolene asks huskily. I have to admit that since switching careers from Blocked Writer to Blocked Writer *therapist*, Jolene is looking good. She seems calmer, slimmer, more rested. Her dangly ethnic earrings and strange paisley leggings look somehow *right* in this setting.

"Uh-huh," the stricken woman says. "I think about how five years ago he wrote this novel, a mystery novel, and the sad thing is . . ." Her hands close into fists. "He never *did* anything with it! Never sent it out to one publisher, to one agent!" Then she shrugs, her tone turning casual. "Sure, the book had problems. It was five hundred pages, some of the sections rambled, he hadn't really bothered to edit it. . . ." The keening timbre returns. "But to just *leave* it! To just never follow *up*, never *do* anything!

"Do you see?" she agonizes. "Because of the *weight* of all this, I find it hard to give myself . . . Permission to Write."

. . . .

I'm sitting in, an invited guest of honor, at Jolene's new Right to Write group. Turning forty-two, in a crisis, she decided to embark on a brand-new career. That is, she has started this support group for bored Westside professionals all around her age who've decided, in the midst of their midlife crises, that what they really want to do is write novels. (At fifty dollars per person per session, it's proven extremely lucrative for Jolene: "Now that I've completely abandoned my *own* writing, I feel happier, healthier, and, my God, my phone never stops ringing!")

And now, after the first testimony, a silence has fallen.

I ponder the female marketing executive's situation. The

unexplained twenty-year break from writing, the hatred of solitude, the chronic revulsion felt when rereading her own pieces.

"There is another possibility," I hear myself saying.

"Yes?" She and the rest of the group lean in. There is a rustle of Ralph Lauren Leisurewear. Eight pairs of eyes look up at me.

I, the Great Blocked Novelist, give my pronouncement.

"Maybe you're *just . . . not . . . a writer.*"

A gasp goes up—particularly from Jolene. She invited me to provide *inspiration.*

But I can't stop myself. What I have to tell them is too important! I stand, begin to witness.

"I myself once had a bad case of Novel Disease—or, as some prefer to call it, Novelitis. For three years, my own dead novel lived in boxes in a locked back bedroom, like the stuffed dead mother rocking in *Psycho.* And yet I *couldn't stop talking about it.* I couldn't stop *telling* people about that cold, dead novel. . . .

"In fact, here's a kind of personal litmus test for you. If you spend more time *complaining* about writing your novel than actually *writing* your novel, guess what? You're *not* a novelist! Plenty of *other* novelists actually *finish* their manuscripts. By contrast, there's *you*, not . . . in that special group.

"By all counts, *Jerry*"—I whirl to face a mournful divorce lawyer in Garrison Keillor glasses, whose sad case Jolene has filled me in on—"eight years is *enough time* to do . . . *a draft*, if the language system is English. Perhaps if you were inventing a *new* language system like, say, a James Joyce, some kind of *Finnegan's Wake*, ten years for a first draft *would* be appropriate, but in that case, you should be showing your group a glossary at least, a vocabulary list, an alphabet. Do you understand? Eight years into this supposed novel, you should be producing *pages . . .* of some kind!"

Jerry takes off his glasses and wipes his eyes, destroyed. And yet somehow, I can't help sensing, relieved. I'm leading the Scared Straight of novel-writing workshops, and it's doing everyone good.

"All of you, UCLA Extension people . . ." I continue. "You

don't want to *write* a novel—you want to put absolutely no effort in and have a novelistic *experience*. Because what you're addicted to is not writing, but writing *workshops*. You snort them up like cocaine. Am I right?" A small Edvard Munch *The Scream*—faced woman in a Laura Ashley dress nods.

I lower my voice, lean in further. They lean in further, too, horrified and yet . . . titillated. "I understand you because I'm an addict myself. Barely reformed. In fact, it's all I can do not to just *run off and join one right now!* Ohhhh yes. Just thinking about crackling open a Brand New Writing Workshop brings a sharp little pang. . . ."

I narrow my eyes onto a distant point, the way I always remember Ruth doing. (I have to say, I'm loving this. The lid has blown off my cave. The flue is open. A million images and ideas are coming to me!)

"The moment the Famous Writer sweeps into that classroom that very first day!" I exclaim, rhapsodically. "The Famous Writer, typically a fabulously shattered-looking person in his late fifties—shattered and yet surprisingly . . . *lean* and *lithe* (yoga?) in his boot-cut jeans and Navajo vest, crowned with silver-shot yet leonine hair.

"The blue-and-white Kinko's bag . . . the crisp cut of pages . . . the circle of pale faces . . . and your first critique! Which is absolutely terrible. The teacher (in little round John Lennon glasses today), as calm and unforgiving as a sheer rock cliff, seems to *see right through you*. 'Sandra,' he announces, in front of the whole room. 'You write facilely, and quickly, but without really *thinking*. It's like you're *afraid, afraid* to go deeper. You might want to think about what makes you so *afraid* . . . to show up . . . on the page.'

"Now comes the biting of the lip," I sweep on, suffused by the drama of it, "the stiff, haughty exodus to the bathroom, collapse onto the floor, sickening whirl of white tile, etc., etc., blah blah blah, four weeks later, new pages, delved deeper, hugs/relief/tears/laughter/cappuccinos. Eddying up from the debris that night is a knot of feisty, like-minded, 'You go, girl!' Sisters (and one guy, a lawyer, Doug)—fabulous, empathic people you want to stay in touch with forever. In fact, here's an idea: 'Let's start our *own* writers' group!'

"Hosting the first meeting, Doug leads a walk-through of his million-dollar home in the Palisades, points out the guest cottage he's remodeling so he can finally have A Quiet Place to Write."

There are murmurs of recognition. The Laura Ashley/*Scream* lady nudges the manqué Garrison Keillor. "Like Randall," she murmurs. "His pool house."

"The pool house, let's say." I smile, patting her hand. She brightens. "Which has . . ." I narrow my eyes, channel the decor. . . .

"Skylights. Exposed beams. Mexican paver tile. View of the Pacific. And is that even . . . a small fireplace? Doug gets to write in front of a fireplace? The rest of you are instantly stricken, try not to show it. When Doug goes on, says his dream is to 'take a year off and write a novel,' it sounds like he's going to visit some wonderful spa . . . like he'll have all the pleasure of curling up before a fire and *reading* a novel, except that now he'll get the added bonus of fame.

" 'I'm just so sick of all the bullshit at the office!' Doug exclaims. 'The politics, the dishonesty, the sheer drudgery of doing the same thing over and over again . . .'

"Of course, as he'd find out—were he to put the years in, which he won't, he'll just get blocked, and use that as an excuse to go to more workshops—that's exactly what being a writer is like.

"Okay? Here comes the tough love. Bend over. Close your eyes."

Hypnotized, they do. I also close my eyes, and speak in deep sonorous tones.

"Take everything horrible about your day job—the repugnantly selfish coworkers (your writers' group), hostile vendors (aloof publishers, agents), kidney-squeezing boredom in the continual pointless loop (that would be called the process of writing), even the manning of a booth for your product at a conference in the fluorescently lit Anaheim Convention Center to which, humiliatingly, no one comes. Multiply by ten and imagine doing that for decades, with

no health insurance and less-than-minimum-wage pay. Voilà: Life of the Writer.

"And don't forget the weariness—the weariness of having to continually restate your life plan: 'I will publish my first novel by the age of twenty-five' shifting to 'I will get my first book contract by the age of thirty—and it can be a nonfiction one' to 'How about at least some decent health insurance by the age of thirty-five' to 'Lots of moisturizing in the new year: It's just about how old you *look!*' It is the weariness of realizing you've been hammering out the same pitiable *Artist's Way* 'morning pages' (a tremulously scrawled 'I need to find the joy again, the *joy*') for months. . . .

"You look around your little home 'office' and the sight of your own neatly cataloged manuscripts, demo tapes, proof sheets, whatever, makes you ill. You have, in that moment, an over-whelming sense that you've been living in your imagination so long, you're even boring yourself.

"Do you guys hear me? I've had purer 'highs' off paying my bills with Quicken!"

"Quicken!" they murmur. Apparently they like Quicken, too.

"As creative people in Los Angeles," I wax on, "I think we all start out sharing the same general life plan, do we not? That is, to be wildly successful at an obscenely young age, to sleep with a lot of famous people, to purchase a skylit house in Laurel Canyon with cash, vague notions about a fashion spread in British *Vogue*.

"As the years drift by, however, you learn most 'careers' unfold more along the following lines:

Sandra's Rules of Artistic Success

1. Any goal you set will take seven to twelve years longer to complete than you'd dreamed it would even at the outside.
2. The money will be approximately one-tenth what you guessed it would be . . . and to your surprise this will really, really bother you.
3. By the time you reach said goal, someone you truly loathe will have reached it a long time ago already.

"You may open your eyes now," I conclude.

"Whew," people in the group are saying, their cheeks flushed, eyes bright with the thrill of going to a support group and ending up being spanked, and hard.

"Put another way," I say. "If 'showing up on the page' is so healing, why have so many of our greatest writers been fall-down-drunk alcoholics? Perhaps it's because no one's buying their books. No: All their potential readers are lounging around in velveteen loveseats in Starbucks, Learning Annex catalogs fanned out in front of them, dreaming about writing their *own* memoirs when they could be at home, reading real writers' books!"

And now I, their abusive guru, come to the real heart of the piece. I join hands with the person on my left, and on my right.

"And now you see the unfolding of my deeper message, my spiritual call to arms. To be blunt, here are the top three global resources getting scarcer in the twenty-first century:

- ozone layer
- rain forest
- people eager to read the fiction of others

"That's right, folks. For the first time in I believe written history, there are far more fiction *writers* on earth than fiction *readers*. How did we get here? Take the self-help movement—which says we should all tell our stories, whether we're 'writers' or not. Add the plunging price of computers—which enable us to print twenty copies of said story and, via yon whining snowmobile of the *Writer's Market*, plow these manuscripts onto the fragile ecosystem of the world's nonprofit literary magazines—magazines we've never bought nor seen, nor do we plan to.

"Indeed, the problem's so bad, literary magazines have developed form letters they send back to would-be authors, in vain attempts to get them to actually *read* the publication. *The Cimmaron Review*: 'If just one out of six people submitting stories to our magazine bought just one annual subscription, we could afford to stay in print!' Gordon Lish: 'Save yourself the postage, save yourself the bother, save yourself the wasted time and the wasted hope—by first earning an *approximate* notion of the manner of attitude underlying the prose and poetry constituting an issue of the *Q.*'

"It's why yon PEN/Faulkner Award winner (boot-cut jeans, leonine hair) is hard-pressed to find fifty people who'll pay twenty-five dollars for his new hardback. However, he has no trouble finding one hundred people who'll pay four hundred dollars to learn to write . . . *fiction!* Which no one will read. Except maybe the students they then take on. See? It's a pyramid scheme!

"In short, there is a serious attention span problem in this country, and if you must write—and I respect that—please write *responsibly.* Consider the fragility of our biosphere. Let's borrow a page from that nasty Gordon Lish. For every twenty manuscripts you send out (five dollars in first-class postage there/back times twenty equals a hundred dollars), you should buy five literary magazines (five dollars times five equals twenty-five dollars). For every writing workshop you take (four hundred dollars), you should buy four books (one hundred dollars). Before you take that year off and write a novel, ask yourself, When's the last time I sat down and *read* one?

"Be very Native American in your thinking. Take only the self-expression you need. Give back where you can.

"On the other hand, if you're the sort of person who, after a long day at work, would rather kick back and watch *Biography,* *watch* it. Enjoy it. Don't feel guilty. By not writing, you're not perpetrating a legacy of silence in your family. You're not stifling your inner child. You're not being commitmentphobic.

"You're just *you* . . . a person who doesn't really enjoy writing. And that's beautiful."

They clap. They hug me. They want to know where to sign up for the next session.

"Instead of 'Right to Write' workshops," Jolene murmurs, "I should start doing 'Just Say No to Writing' workshops. 'Scared Straight from Writing.' Or 'Novel-Anon.' "

"Good idea," I say. "And count me in, dammit! I'm starting to feel really unblocked! I could do this all day!" And indeed, I seem to have found my calling. Giving really, really abusive advice to people. I could write my own anti–self help book!

November 14

```
TO:      Everyone
FROM:    Sandra
RE:      Upcoming Holidays
DATE:    November 14
```

Dear Everyone,

Yes, the boycott is over. I will indeed be coming
home for Thanksgiving/Christmas/New Year's/etc.
this year. Personal note: I have recently made
the decision to hand all my finances over to
Kaitlin, who seems to have more than enough time/
energy/tragically unused brain cells to get me
more of a 16 percent yield instead of a 4 percent
yield over a twenty-year period with far greater
liquidity and far less load on a government-
insured SEP-IRA or something like that.

Sitting in Kaitlin's bank, which is brand-spanking
new and sleek and terrific and indeed full of
wonderful, innovative customer-service programs,
enjoying my free cappuccino and biscottis and
also some pens, I got to thinking how in a way
our very family is like a corporation (with a
board, and employees, and part-time temps, and
everything like that). And that perhaps the family communications should be treated as such.

To that end, I have drawn up the following inter-
personal memo that I believe you will all find
extremely helpful. If only in the sense that you
can see how truly crazy I've become and therefore
how much all of you need, this holiday, to cut me
a lot of, lot of, lot of slack.

<attachments>

Christmas: New Technology

Open Memo, cc: Everyone

As we family members gingerly lower ourselves
into our starting blocks for the traditional,
grueling, eight-hundred-yard run that is the
holidays, the more *progressive* of us might wonder
(much like the Bank of America or Wells Fargo):

What, in some small way, can we--as a team--
do *better* this year? How, without changing our
management structure, may we provide one another
with better family *service*--quicker, more
focused, more responsive? Can some of the traditional family end-of-the-year bumps/snafus/
foobars/ghost service charges/*penalties* even,
be *eliminated*, or at least *minimized*?

Personally, I think so. Unlike others, I do not
feel that, within our family, the occasional
holiday misreadings/misunderstandings/keening
outbursts/emotional breakdowns/full-on train
wrecks are to be blamed on specific *individuals,*
some of whose very continued tenure *within* the
organization, at remote sites, several weeping
hours' drive from the explosion area, is annually
questioned.

No, I take the tack that differences among various family members are to be *celebrated*. Decades
of exhaustive research (and periodic experimen-
tal interventions) indicate that no one is ever
going to *change.* Therefore I believe, to ensure
a more satisfying holiday experience, we need to
look at the outdated eighties, seventies, six-
ties, and even fifties family paradigms we may be
hanging on to. To these may be attributed the
setting of unrealistic goals, and the sloppy way
crucial information is often disseminated.

**1. Update on What We Do the Other 346 Days
of the Year**

To that last end, I propose we kick off the
upcoming Thanksgiving holiday with a quick thirty-
minute orientation--or, I should say, *reorienta-
tion*--on Who We Currently Are. Our lives, our
jobs--what we actually *do,* for instance, all day,
at the office. It *seems,* so often, we annually
re-brief others on this basic information, and
annually, they *re-forget.*

Kaitlin, the eldest sister, has submitted--and I
think it's a good point--that literally *decades*

into her job, her family members still have absolutely no idea what she does. They cannot even
name her title. To help us, Kaitlin writes:

"For the last time. I am co-executive adminis-
trative director of the Helton-Ross Dynamic
Fund for Northern California Privately-Invested
Non-Profit Corporations. Okay? I make money for
people. I make money. Our vice-president, who
I'm always annoyed with, every year, since 1993,
is named Gerald. Because Gerald has a problem
with delegation. De-le-gation."

Some of you, rather than merely tuning out the
current Who We Are, seem to be clinging to *outdated* versions. One of you, for instance, is
still trying to operate Sandra 1.0, a thing that
has been obsolete for many, many, many years.
It is a version that does not even run on the new
Sandra. For the record, Papa, I am *not* "on hiatus"
from grad school. I actually dropped out of the
graduate program at USC eight years ago. Eight.
Let's print it on a card. Put a little chain
on it. You can wear it around your wrist like a
medical bracelet. Which is what you'll need when
we hurl your nonlistening body into which no new
information can ever penetrate onto the porch.
Onto the porch.

As for my "looking tired," Papa? I don't want to
give anything away, but . . . I think you'll be
pleasantly surprised.

2. Games and Activities of the Holidays

Typically, the advent of the endless Christmas
holiday has meant one thing: groups of people
sitting around in their sweatpants in a living
room with the thermostat turned up way too high
for days . . . and days . . . and days.

Let's face it. No matter how interesting we all
are, if you happen to be in a family that isn't
fighting (as ours currently isn't), the action

can get pretty slow between December 22 and January 3. It's just . . . too much time to be together. I mean, we can update one another in forty-eight hours. Three meals together and we're totally up to speed: how much sleep we're getting, how much work we're doing, what our finances are, etc., etc.

There will be afternoon-length monologues about bad bosses, baby photo albums four inches thick, unintelligible blueprints for future kitchen remodelings. After that will begin the slide into reheated decaf, watching TV while pretending not to, watching obscenely boring home video of people actually present *watching* TV, say four months ago, when the video camera was new, before they got their bangs cut, and eating pie.

Let us take a bold step forward. Let us be the sort of fabulous, shining, forward-thinking Family 2000 (F-2000) *not* in Denial about how boring we are. By Day Three, let's have photo albums stashed, gifts cleared away, and the Scrabble out. The talking is done. (It's like, you listened to my problems, I listened to yours, there's nothing I can do, you never listen to advice I give you anyway, but it's okay with me, I've been in therapy, pick some letters.)

Others may, as they do annually, proffer other games. But let's be realistic.

Boggle is stressful.

Scruples causes fights. WIFE: "If you were run- ning late, of *course* you'd park in a handicapped space for two minutes." HUSBAND: "I'd *never* do that. *You're* the one who'd do that!"

Monopoly is fun, but brings up money. In Christ- mas 1991, when Cousin Stanley famously demanded, "Hotel on Park Place! You owe me three thousand dollars! You owe me three thousand dollars!" I turned into a seven-year-old and started to cry. I was temping that year and feeling fragile.

Cards are good, especially if you never make spouses partners. However, this terrible thing has happened in the land where no one knows the same card games anymore. Some people know Hearts, others Pinochle, Smear, Bridge. That is, they know them, but not well enough to explain the rules to others. This seems to trigger more unintelligible monologues.

"It's like . . . Jacks? They're high. But not with a ten. See? Not with a ten. Because Julie played the Queen of Spades. That's the exception I told you about. Also the Joker. When you don't have the two. Because even when hearts are trump, Queen of Spades leads. Because she's the Black Lady. She's the Black Lady."

And everyone's going . . . what? Is he nuts?

The beauty of Scrabble is that those *not* in the fold can soon be brought *into* the fold. When a novice sister-in-law exclaims, "My letters are *terrible!* A *J* and an *X*? What can I spell with *these?*" one of our goons, our family henchpeople, can be dispatched to instruct her.

That person shall receive the following small Care package of two-letter words:

j-o--Scottish word for sweetheart
x-i--spelling of the Greek letter xi
l-i--Chinese currency

This is enough to give them the idea for others. Some argue, esoterically, that these are also acceptable:

a-e--Hawaiian for lava
a-i--a three-toed sloth

But their opponents argue that these are from the Scrabble dictionary. Which is not a real dictionary. It's the sort of dictionary where they make *up* words to keep selling Scrabble boards! From the Hawaiian? From the Greek? Where are we: Fiji? There have been many ugly eruptions over this, so . . . let's just say no.

However, weirdly enough, due to a great lack of
Z words, everyone seems to agree on and enjoy
"ziti," and also its erstwhile plural, "zitis"
(aka *many* Italian pastas). So for this year,
until further notice, "zitis" is okay.

3. The Grisly Matter of Gifting

Let's face it: The gift-giving ante has risen
high in these past few decades. Perhaps too high.
I for one am exhausted. Gone are the days when
one could lob plutonium-hard fruitcakes over the
gates of one's enemies. When a woman could give
her man an ugly tie or pine-scented cologne,
because she knew all she'd ever get back was a
collection of weird little soaps or a tire iron.

Those were simpler times, when a bottle of
peppermint schnapps was fine for an uncle, Mon
Cheri candies for the daughter-in-law, five bucks
for someone's little nephew Ricky. When it was
understood that most of these things would either
be ritually tossed or passed on to Scotty the
lecherous gas-meter man in the great circle of
unwanted holiday gift-giving. But no. Try spread-
ing a little of that kind of cheer in the family
today, and you'll get a punch in the nose. Or
worse, the gift returned, with a woeful tale of
dysfunction . . .

How Timothy's wife has a drinking disorder and
therefore cannot tolerate any alcohol in the
home. How Narda Lynn, the girlfriend of the
college-aged cousin, nonsmoker, vegetarian,
M.A. in Comp Lit from Brown, quite proficient
in Windows 95, is allergic to sugar (is that
even possible?). How little Ricky's parents
do not believe in cash gifts for kids because
"we're trying to wean Richard off a legacy of
entitlement."

In this new millennium, no wonder we've come to
eye the gift-giving process with a sullen weari-

ness, as we would some complex digital technology
spun out of control.

The problem, it seems, is that two new gift-giving
rituals have entered our social lexicon, i.e.,

1. The delivering of the morality lecture
2. The bursting into tears

Or they may combine. This is particularly so when
one is handed a gift one doesn't like--which in
the old days, remember, was par for the course.
But no. Today we feel we need to complicate mat-
ters with sentiments like:

* "You really thought . . . I would like this."
* "Don't you know that teak is endangered?"
* "Why do you always go so crazy at Christmas?
  What's so difficult about a monthly phone
  call *during the year?*"

Then again, perhaps worse are those whose emo-
tions are so repressed, their only outlet for
expressing disappointment is via the gift itself.
For example:

* "I have donated fifty dollars in your name to
  the ACLU."
* "This is called an Abdominizer."
* "We can't use this Scotch. Probably you can."

No wonder as the year draws to a close, sensing
thunderclouds ahead, families try to be proactive. I am hearing a lot today about annual
post-Thanksgiving discussions and retreats.
Arguments are heard. Votes are taken. An annual
mission statement is drafted, distributed by
mother via form letter: "Everyone picks a name
out of a hat." "No gift over twenty-five dollars." "2002 signals a moratorium on bears or
bear-themed items."

To which I say: Forget it. Merry Christmas.
Here's your fruitcake. You know what to do
with it.

4. Explanation About the Rubber Plates

In the past, thanks to the efforts of dear Tante
Lotte, we have had the tradition of always eating
emotion-fraught holiday meals on, yes, the fine
family china, each fragile piece a landmine,
waiting to go off. Here is a thing that comes
from a tiny European town (Keshlooponslesen!)
that was so lovely, so magical (laughing, dancing, violins) before it was tragically *bombed*--
but before it was *bombed,* there was a little tiny
uncle who made this saucer upon which he hand-
embossed the family name in the thinnest line
of gold--

And let us say there is a bewildering *amount* of
this china for people who dine on eleven tiny
courses. There is the beschlerpuppsleber! for
the asparagus and the klinghouflasser! for the
brussels sprouts, and hand-washing these one
hundred-plus pieces is like dental surgery, and
who does this duty fall to? Sullen teenagers.
Sul-len teenagers. Snapping gum. Loading the
dishwasher. Pickin' up the steel wool. Steel
wool. "Hey, man--what does this do?"

I say, let us continue to saw apart turkey on
emotion-laden symbols of irrevocable family
loss, but let's focus on ancestors who made fine,
hand-crafted *rubber* objects. The Tupperware people. The Plastic Laminates. The Scotch Guard.
Maybe then we'll get to actually digest.

January 1

11:47 a.m.

Temperature: 72 degrees,
Wet, Right After a Thunderstorm

Van Nuys, California

●

After Just Having Returned from Carmel, California,

The Most Beautiful Place on Earth . . .

Except for the Fact That My Family Lives There

(Because you know what, friends?

No matter how perfect a town *looks*, there's always *something* . . .)

●

Paradise

know we sometimes feel as though we hate where we live. However, after spending a grisly holiday away, my eyes have been
opened.

Of course, it's true that I happen to live in my hometown's,
Los Angeles's, most verdant and lovely part: Van Nuys, yon bosom
of green. I awake this morning, after the archetypal horrendous,
overbooked, holiday coach flight like a bat out of SFO, not Tower
Air exactly but an experience that was very Tower-*like*—here,
let us strip in the stock footage: lines of refugees, screaming children, Hanoi: the bombing of, etc.

Anyway, I awake this morning in my own bed, look out at a
gentle curtain of warm rain trembling on chlorophyll-swollen
leaves and waterlogged hibiscus, and I think, Where am I? Van
Nuys? Or the *island* of *Maui?*

Newly curious, I slip into a pair of plastic flip-flops and
slide into my sun-beaten/rain-washed/naturally-weathered-as-
a-great-head-on-Easter-Island Honda. I am still in the T-shirt
and shorts I slept in, as is the custom on our little atoll so many
sailing days north of Ventura Boulevard. I turn the car up Hazeltine to navigate the customary half-block to the corner minimall
to get milk for our morning coffee.

Up above me spreads the great white sky. To my left and to my
right are quaint residential bungalows in their familiar hues of
lime green, raspberry cream, banana yellow, all the colors of the
rainbow. . . .

"I know where I am," I correct myself. "I'm in Mexico! In the little tropical Mexican town that is my—"

But no, I realize. This is not Mexico, it is not Maui, it is not anywhere but Van Nuys. This eerie outpost, oddly radiant in the post-thunderstorm light. This strange little corner with no rules and, yet, a multitude of glamorous possibilities. . . .

After all, Provence is here, the Congo is here, even Oglala Springs is here.

Why? Because for me, they exist in only one place. In my imagination. Which lives . . . right here on this block.

As the "Shop Here Food Mart" door jingles closed behind me, I am newly struck with awe. Hard to say which is the more amazing to my travel-wearied eyes: (a) the sheer surplus of square footage in the place, some of the shelves sitting nearly empty, or (b) the absence of any shred of current media or world news. No: The small magazine rack features only a stack of *Auto-buys* and a lone, yellowed August *Vogue*. I am in heaven, I think.

I get the milk, I get back in the car, and, drifting lazily south on Hazeltine, I reflect on what has happened in the last year. . . .

I began unemployed. I'm still unemployed.

I began without a career. I still don't have a career.

I began married. I'm still married.

However, because twelve months have passed, it's fair to say that the mortgage on our rat hole . . . is just a little bit smaller.

Overall, it's a year in which *nothing major* happened. Nothing major was accomplished. On the Gains vs. Losses sheet of life, we're at less than a tie.

And yet, and yet, and yet . . . I can't help shaking this vague, vague sense that, like the proverbial curl of distant woodsmoke glimpsed faintly over a hill, there was a germ of a story somewhere in there. . . .

I look away. Look back. The thin, lazy curl of the story is still there.

Inviting—

But because I've chased and scared off *so* many good ideas before, for a moment, I'll let it be. I'll leave it in its lazy state of promise.

There's no rush. Not anymore.

Because, no longer officially one of the Young, or the Fresh, or the Promising, with all their schedules and rules and urgency, with absolutely no one watching me or judging me or even giving a flying fuck what I do anymore, I suddenly find I have . . . all the time in the world. And miles of blue road stretch ahead.

And so, I step out of the cracked dead shell of my Youth, and older, yet oddly lighter, I set off.

Acknowledgments

The author wishes to thank the following:

Ruth Seymour and KCRW (Los Angeles) for the gift of radio time and space, and also all the swinging hipsters at Marketplace (PRI); Cathy Seipp for the title; Sloan Harris for his gentle ministrations; Doug Pepper for his enormous verve and style; The Warriors Within, aka my writing group—Cassandra Clark, Samantha Dunn, and Beverly Olevin—for their excellent editorial comments, and hummus. For witticisms either purloined or inspired: Andy Berkin, Tom Christie, Peter Coward (TM), Julian (hugs/tears/cappuccinos) Fleischer, John Forker, Mel Green, Fred Paroutaud, and—always a sight for sore eyes—the eternally youthful David "Peter Pan" Schweizer. Helpful female spirits along life's way: "Beverly Kaye and Associates!," Jackie Shepperson, Buddhist Mary South, Vicki Wood and her Forty Thieves, Donna Dees for generously sharing the files and correspondence of Ms. Virginia Tobin. Model couples in or out of pie charts: the beautifully wedded Tom Bryant and Ann Richardson, Jimmy Johnson and Leslie Nitta, Adam Shulman and Mark Litwin, Helen and Mike Clinco for the Gravy. And of course Susan Marder (who does not in any way resemble Bert Lahr) and Rich Ruttenburg, for many great New Years and multiple Paul Williams sightings at Petco (not to mention the surprising bonus of Morgan Fairchild at Bed, Bath and Beyond).

Thank you, Danny Rubin.

Thank you, Irene Lacher.

Thank you, Renee Vogel, the molecular opposite of anything Amelia.com.

Thank you, Mark Salzman and Jessica Yu for, at the very *least*, some fantastically catastrophic vacation reading materials: *Mexico in 2005!*

Thank you, Henry Alford, a human more delectable than even Vermont's tiniest jam.

Hats off to the mysteriously enigmatic Eugene Loh Jr., wife Judy Griffith, and their three young'uns, who grow and flourish so beautifully outside of literature. And thanks to Mike Miller, the world's funniest person with whom to discuss things one shouldn't have eaten, who will never challenge the word "zitis" in Scrabble (although, trust me, he will almost everything else).